Supernatural Assault in Ancient Egypt

Seth, Evil Sleep & The Egyptian Vampire

by Mogg Morgan

Mandrake

Copyright © Mogg Morgan and Mandrake of Oxford, 2011
Second edition

All rights reserved. No part of this work may be reproduced or utilized in any form by any means electronic or mechanical, including *xerography, photocopying, microfilm*, and *recording*, or by any information storage system without permission in writing from the author.

Published by
Mandrake of Oxford
PO Box 250
OXFORD
OX1 1AP (UK)

A CIP catalogue record for this book is available from the British Library and the US Library of Congress.

ISBN 978-1-906958-32-9

*   The Egyptian language consistently ignored vowels so by convention and for convenience of pronounciation English vowel 'e' is inserted between each consonant apart from ʿ & ꜣ where 'a' is pronounced as in French.

Contents

Chapter 1	The Kiss of the Vampire:	7
	The 'evil sleep' of Egyptian Magick	7
	The night terrors	9
	Ankhew, the Akhew and the Neterew	10
	Egyptian Ka & Ba	18
	The Ban of the Bori	19
	The Blue Lily	28
	More on the Akhw	36
Chapter 2	An Egyptian origin for the European Vampire myth	43
	Jacob's Ladder	50
Chapter 3	Egyptian Psychology	55
	Egyptian personalities	58
	The God in him is Horus	58
	The God in him is Seth	60
	The Goddess in her is Isis	62
	The Goddess in her is Nephthys.	65
	Appendix: A dream manual	71
Chapter 4	Lucky and Unlucky	82
	Appendix: Almanac	98
Chapter 5	Supernatural assault	145
	Bibliography	159
	Glossary	171
	Index	183

Figures

Figure 1:   Astronomical ceiling from tomb of Seti I 6
Figure 2:   Ostraca Gardiner 363 - Front and Back 11
Figure 3:   The Akh or Crested Ibis 23
Figure 4:   The Panacht Stele 27
Figure 5:   20th Dynasty granite statue of Seth 33
Figure 6:   Painting (with details) of blue faience chalice 35
Figure 7:   Images of Seth in canid form 51
Figure 8:   Nerinea DeFrance 52
Figure 9:   Symbol of the Rekhyt, the folk 64
Figure 10: Menit showing gods of the Decans 84
Figure 11: Papyrus text of an amuletic decree 86
Figure 12: Wooden container for an Amulet 87
Figure 13: Papyrus London-Leiden 23/1-20. 147
Figure 14: Wooden Akh from Deir el-Medina, ... 151
Figure 15: Akh - another example 155

Tables

Table 1:   The Dreams of the Horus & Sethian types 71-81

Evil Sleep

You're in your bed, it's dark, you hear footsteps coming up the stairs and into your room. There's someone there - a presence. They lie on you or beside you, perhaps even gripping you tightly, crushing you into the bed. You can't move. There may be a sound, a grunt or a strange smell. Time passes, you are paralysed with fear. Eventually the entity changes, perhaps expanding or contracting, moving away from you, sinking to the floor. With a great effort of will you manage to move the tip of your finger, then the hand until movement returns to your whole body and the experience ends. You have been visited by the old 'hag'.

Inspired by: *The Terror that Comes in the Night: An experience centred study of supernatural assault traditions,* Hufford 1982

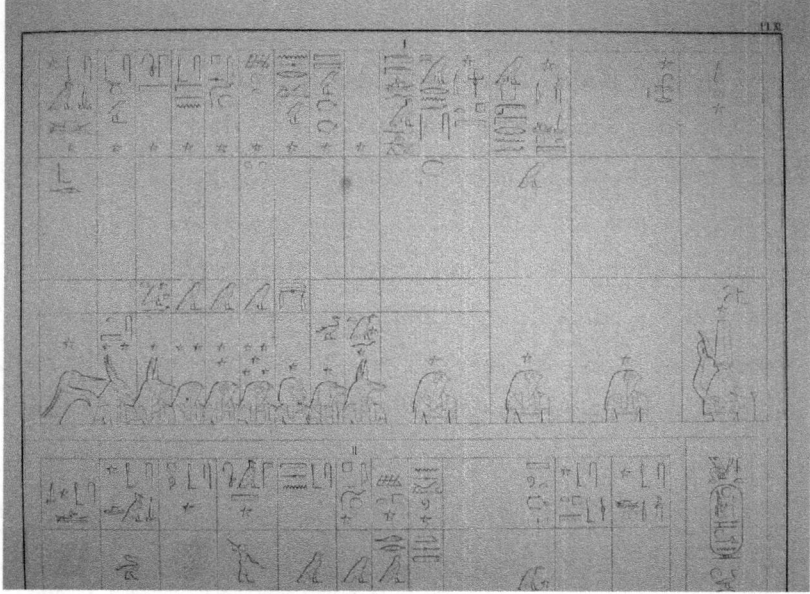

Figure 1: Vaulted astronomical (detail) from the ceiling, Hall K of the tomb of Seti I in the Valley of the Kings, Luxor. xix dynasty 1302 - 1290 BCE. The above drawing made by Lefébure in 1884 shows a portion of the list of planets and triangular decans now missing. The original is solid blue with figures in yellow with red outlines. The Heron on the left represents Osiris in his aspect as the planet Venus (Seba-Da). Second from the left is Seth in his aspect as Mercury (Sebegew). Next come triangular decans.[1]

1. The Kiss of the Vampire:

The 'evil sleep' of Egyptian Magick

'The night was man's first necessary evil,
our oldest and most haunting terror'
from A Roger Ekirch (2005) *At Day's Close* [2]

Our preliminary study of ancient lunar symbolism leads naturally enough to the activities of the night, an area that has an unexpected and largely ignored history. Until the advent of efficient lighting, human activity largely stopped at sun-down, to begin again just before dawn. This was especially true on moonless nights. It is widely supposed that the night was always a source of fear, the domain of frightening and threatening entities.

Thus Plato wrote: 'Evil spirits love not the smell of lamps.' It may be as well to remind ourselves that the humble lamp, that we take so much for granted, had in the ancient world wider connotations as a complex magical instrument with which the huddling masses did battle with the monsters from the Id.

So in what follows I want to discuss some of the Ancient Egyptian responses to the terrors of the night. This will bring us into the realm of ancient psychology and demonology. It will also reveal the domain of private, freeform, improvised Egyptian magick and witchcraft. It will cause us to read the most ancient of dream books, and also look at *Almanacs of Lucky and Unlucky days* (wrongly called 'calendars' by some cursory readers). It will uncover some hardcore spell kits designed to fight 'evil' with 'evil'.[3]

I should say that I approach this material as a practitioner of magick rather than as a disinterested academic. Some might say I am part of the new breed of scholar-practitioners. We have a unique point of view often drawn to the material by mysterious forces - spiritual quests, that kind of thing. For me personally, I have had a longstanding obsession with the supposed 'dark side' of hermeticism and the occult. My obsession has compelled me to study the secret byways of ancient magick. I believe that certain things have been revealed to me. But I also know that no one is going to take that seriously unless I can provide hard evidence for my interpretations, some of which can seem wildly at odds with 'accepted wisdom'.

When looking at magical material, including the Egyptian, it is as well to bear in mind that it is only in the last few decades that this has received any proper analysis. The magical practitioner now takes a more objective, empirical approach. Put in a nutshell, we all got so bored of listening to so-called experts misinterpreting our religion that we thought that we could do a better job ourselves - and this has largely turned out to be the case. The current vast growth in new material is probably the direct result of this sea change. In consequence it means that a great deal of material written before the 1980s needs looking at again. In fact it has been said that academics and archaeologists were once in the habit of digging up material then preparing it for swift reburial. I give several examples of this in my book the *Bull of Ombos*, and almost all of the texts discussed below have suffered a similar fate.

What follows is 'work in progress' for a small group of contemporary magicians experimenting with the material to see if it can still be relevant to the 21st century.

The night terrors

I am going to look at an artifact that provoked a decisive debate, leading to the 'victory' of 'pagan' Egyptologists over their 'Christian' protagonists. It happens to be an ancient spell against night terrors. In the 1990s, the award winning scholar Robert Ritner wrote a short article discussing this strange artifact. What he said changed many people's view of Egyptian magick. Previously, Egyptian magick was seen as very formal, the province only of the temple.

We modern practitioners once saw Egyptian magick through the prism of the Hermetic Order of the Golden Dawn. Our rituals were full of long, obscure speeches and elaborate costumes. The reconstruction of Egyptian magick as practiced in the Hermetic Order of the Golden Dawn was heavily influenced by Wallis Budge. Budge's voluminous and widely available books are nowadays considered very out of date. And indeed the con-temporary practitioner has also tired of the theatrical version of Egyptian and classical magick. Contemporary magick is much more interested by what's going on inside our heads, much more interested in what the ancients called *gnosis*.

I opened this chapter with a reference to a modern study of

supernatural assault traditions. The kind of phenomena studied in Professor Hufford's book, is pretty much the same as Egyptian experience of 'evil sleep'.[4] Such experiences continue to plague us, regardless of whether we live our lives in sleepy backwaters or cutting-edge metropolitan communities. Research shows that almost everyone will experience sleep paralyis at some point in their lives. With this in mind we can perhaps more fully appreciate the kind of responses made to the same phenomenon by our Egyptian forebears. Lest you think this topic is totally negative can we agree that therapy presupposes some knowledge of pathology?

Ankhew, the Akhew and the Neterew

The ancient Egyptian recognised three categories of sentient beings: The Ankhew, the Akhew and the Neterew which can be translated as the Living, the Dead and the Gods. All three have their good and bad sides.

There is quite a lot of information to be had concerning the ancient Egyptian fear of attack from night demons. But, because of a general prejudice amongst old guard Egyptologists, much of this information is buried in obscure academic publications. One of these ancient spells is found among a category of artifacts known as *Ostraca*. These are basically fragments of stone or pieces of broken pottery that people in the ancient world used as a convenient form of notepaper.

Bear in mind that papyrus paper was an expensive luxury subject to a royal monopoly. So for humbler, more day to day use, ostraca was the norm. Ostraca are also one of the materials of choice for

SUPERNATURAL ASSAULT IN ANCIENT EGYPT

Figure 2: Ostraca Gardiner 363 - Front and Back

the activities of ancient magick. This is in addition to its convenience as 'note paper'. The material, the actual stone or piece of broken pot probably has ritual significance.

The standard collection of ostraca was compiled by eminent Egyptologists Sir Alan Gardiner and J Cerny in the 1950s.[5] One in particular is important in our study - the very brief entry for Ostraca HO109 reads:

> 'O Gardiner 363. Limestone, inscribed on both sides, but on verso only a few signs are left. Perhaps complete except on left side and at bottom; on the left not much can be lost because of the thinness of the stone at this point. The writing is faint in places. A magical spell.'

It was considered a small object of no great interest and of no relevance to the high culture of Ancient Egypt. Its apparent crudeness marked it out as the work of uneducated folk who worked in the Ramesside colony of craftsmen at Deir el-Medina. It was yet further evidence that these rude working people were largely ignorant of Egyptian religion and theology. It thus lay untranslated for the next thirty years until in 1990 Robert Ritner, an expert of Ancient Egyptian magick, took another look.

To paraphrase his translation:
Oh male adversary (*ḏȝy*),
Oh female adversary,
Oh male ghost,
Oh female ghost

Oh dead men,
Oh dead women,
be far from me.
Listen but do not come.
your faces are twisted backwards
your limbs are unsound.
Your heart is destined for the sacrificial meal
of the Cobra Goddess.
NN born of NN has extracted your hearts,
Oh dead ones.
He has taken your hearts,
Oh dead men and dead women.
You shall be eaten by the Cobra Goddess
and shall not live
Your limbs are offering cakes.
You will not escape the four noble ladies
You will not escape the fortress of Horus Imy Senwet [6]

This spell was to be recited over four nightlights in the shape of cobras and fashioned from pure clay 'with flames in their mouths'. Baked red clay can be regarded as a Sethian ritual material. Each lamp is placed at each corner of every room or any bedroom in which a man or woman are sleeping together. This later perhaps indicated that the perils of the night are related to sexual activity.

Looking at the picture of the ostraca we could almost see it as an ancient Egyptian spellkit containing as it does both the spell and instructions for use. There's a lot to be said about this seemingly boring and unassuming little object:

The theology is totally orthodox

For example consider the protective role of the cobra goddesses employed at the four cardinal directions to defend the boundary of the bedroom. This is a very common motif in Egyptian iconography. In later times whole cities were protected by such entities. For example the *Agathadaemon* of the Ptolemaic city of Alexandria was Isis in her form as a cobra goddess. And this notion of cardinality continues into modern magical practice - where for example suitable entities such as archangels are employed to repell assault from any quarter.

This spell is for *private* use.

This spell did *not* originate as part of a temple ritual. It is one of the earliest known examples of such a *private* spell. Its private nature reveals what we might call the 'freeform' or improvised nature of Egyptian magick.

Temple practice *copies* private ritual

Although this spell is for private use - its techniques are copied in later temple practice. We can therefore surmise that temple ritual is *derived* from *private* spellcraft of the kind seen in this example.

This view of the relationship between the 'folk' and 'priestly' traditions may be controversial for some. It may also be at odds with popular writing on Egyptian magick. But it seems common sense to me. Consider for a moment the events following the reign of Akhenaten.

Akhenaten is sometimes known as a heretic or fanatic because of his persecution of the cults of Amun and to a lesser extent other traditional Egyptian cults. This persecution led to an unexpected reaction. It provoked the emergence (or reemergence) of *personal piety* or *personal* religion. Afterall, if you can't worship your own god because the temple is shut - then you must rely on personal piety which will include insights from the 'folk' (rekhyt) tradition. Consider for a moment the words of this lovely poem of the time:

> My heart longs for the sight of you,
> O lord of the persea tree,
> When your neck receives garlands
> You grant satiation without eating,
> and drunkenness without drinking.
> My heart longs to see you,
> Joy of my heart.
> Amun, champion of the poor
> You are the father of the motherless,
> The husband of the widow.
> How lovely it is to speak your name:
> It is like the taste of life,
> Like a garment for the naked,
> Like the scent of a flowering twig
> At the time of summer's heat...
> Like a breath of air for him who was imprisoned.[8]

Other examples of this process can be seen in the popular consultation of oracles. Archaeological and textual evidence shows that oracles began their life *outside* of the temple enclosures. The activity was so popular that priestly elites soon brought it into the temple. And what began as a folk practice became the *defining* temple ritual. On festival days the image of the god was taken out of its secret shrine and paraded before the people. This very immediate and popular rite allowed the folk (rekhyt) to petition the god and get a direct answer. To explore this issue further I recommend Jan Assmann's *Search for God in Ancient Egypt*.

The role of the priest

Apparently only about 1% of ancient Egyptians could read.[9] Spells such as the one quoted earlier required recitation everyday. This task may have fallen to a temple priest, perhaps a *hery heb* or lector priest - i.e. any literate official who recites spells and rites in the temple or at funerals and assists the panther skin clad Sem priest. These priests were the principle practitioners of magic and medicine. Whether a priest attended every night seems doubtful to me.

The dreamy night air

The spell reveals the way most Egyptians viewed the perils of the night. It reveals a relationship between dangerous disease entities and certain kinds of illness. Central to the process are night demons, 'vampiric' entities that are known to us now as incubi or succubi. These creatures attack sexually entering the body of their victims - perhaps during lovemaking - taking sexual and other body fluids such as blood.

Egyptian demons are not a completely separate species. They come from the same familiar categories of - the living, the dead or the gods. Egyptian demons can be minor dieties bullied into doing unpleasant tasks by the big gods. It is possible that this category of god/demon was particularly fearful to the ordinary folk who were often quite afraid of the gods who lived in the temple. But broadly speaking the demons fall into two broad camps.

i. Those that are emanations of the well known gods and goddesses of Egypt.
ii. Those that are related to the world of men.

Of those related to the gods one of the most common is related to the moon god Khonsu. Almost as common are those related to the goddess Hathor in the form of the so-called Seven Hathors. The Hayety *(h3y.ty)* demon was the emissary of Hathor or the Shemay *(šm3.y)* demon - emissary of Bastet. For most Ancient Egyptians the world of the emissaries was far more real and immediate than that of the abstract gods whose cult is only kept alive by the temple priests. These entities were widely feared throughout Egypt. Left to their own devices they could determines a person's fate at birth, writing it down in Hathor's *Great Book of Fate*. When the time comes, Hathor sends her emissaries or 'flower cutters' to reap that day's harvest of souls:

> 'Then the seven Hathors came to see her and said with one voice "It is by the ('executioner's) blade that she shall die" '
>
> *Tale of Two Brothers*

> 'Presently the Hathors came to determine a fate for him and said "He shall die through a crocodile, or a snake or even a dog".'
>
> *Tale of the Doomed Prince*

Another great category of demon were spirits of place, heaven, earth but especially water.

The words used to denote demon might be better rendered as Greek *Daemona*. Occultists often describe a spiritual entity known as the Holy Guardian Angel, that is attached or comes into existence at our birth or conception.

Egyptian Ka & Ba

The Ka has no clear modern equivalent. At its root is an entity's generative force, thus it lends its meaning to words such as phallus, vulva, rampant bull etc. Ka is the divine creative force that every entity possesses and that ultimately comes down to us from our ancestral spirits. [10]

Closely related to Ka is the Ba, represented as a human headed bird. Some see it as the equivalent of the western term 'soul'; Sanskrit 'Self' or 'Jiva'. The Ba seems to come into existence at a person's birth and cannot then be destroyed, ultimately becoming one of the imperishable stars.

The bodies (djet) of the gods are guaranteed to be imperishable. Whereas our mortal bodies (khet) are corruptible, rotting away after death.

Some people also avoid complete putrefaction and dissolution. They are initiated into a new life as spiritualised or transfigured beings called the Akhw - the 'undead'. For this to happen the deceased needs to be initiated or *spiritualised* - sakh (*s3ḥ*) into a secret knowledge. It has to be *made* to happen using special magical rites. It is a mode of existence pertaining to the next world or the beyond and if not properly understood is capable of causing a lot of trouble. Thus the Akhw were often feared by the ancient Egyptians.

The classes of Akhw

1. Gods, primarily Atum, who in mythology is said to be the creator of gods (Neterw) and Akhw.
2. Minor gods, such as Aken or Nemty (a form of Seth) the custodian of the celestial ferry boat.
3. Unspecified entities such as the four sons of Horus or Seth.
4. The deceased.

The last two are almost always malevolent.
I would add a fifth class viz:
5. The spiritual entity that attaches itself to every individual at birth.

The Ban of the Bori

Egyptologists often look to the *Hausa* people of West Africa & Sudan for insights into Ancient Egypt. Some even say the very term 'Hausa' derives from one of the Pharaohs. In the early part of the twentieth century the anthropologist A J N Treamearne studied the Hausa and their customs publishing his research in a wonderfully titled book - *The Ban of Bori: Demons and Demon Dancing in West & North Africa*.[11]

An ecstatic cult of the Bori is still popular amongst the Hausa populations. The Bori are an array of 'demons', disease entities and nature spirits that amongst other things abhor iron but love dancing. The Bori could be derived from the Egyptian Ba, meaning 'spirit'. Familial groups also have animal totems such as birds and most famously the leopards as in the 'leopard societies'. Treamearne's classic study is still the principle source for this work and it is a moot point as to how these cultures fared throughout the rest of that turbulent century.

The Hausa practiced 'king killing' - ie selected members of the tribe are elevated for a specific period of time, perhaps as long as seven years, at the end of which they are symbolically deposed or sacrificed. This is an extremely archaic survival that clearly once involved some kind of human sacrifice. Tremearne's informants reported that within living memory actual sacrifices had occured and included a ritual meal during which the victim's brain (or animal substitute) was consumed by the participants. Treamearne recognised many ancient precedents to this, including some from English folklore whereby the clergy were required to 'eat' the 'dying breath' of other clergy. It is possible to chart a theoretical chain of transmission of these ideas back to their Egyptian homeland. This, the *Bible* (Numbers xxiii 24) records the traces of the practice of ritual cannibalism: 'For there is no enchantment against Jacob and no divination against Israel . . . Behold, a people! As a lioness it rises up and as a lion it lifts itself; and it does not lie down till it devours the prey and drinks the blood of the slain . . . God brings him out of Egypt; he has as it were the horns of the wild ox, he shall eat up the nations his adversaries and shall break their bones in pieces.' This theme is explored more fully in my book *The Bull of Ombos*.

The Hausa believe that every person is connected with a Bori spirit of the *opposite* sex at birth. Similar beliefs thrive within contemporary occultism where such a spiritual entity is known as the Holy Guardian Angel. Such entities are often said to attach themselves or come into existence at one's birth or conception.

The Hausa engage in relationships with this spirit throughout their entire life, certainly until they marry. Marriage is often a crisis point when the person must change the focus of their affections. This is a partial explanation for the numerous folk customs associated with marriage - for example the wearing of the veil and companionship of bridesmaids which all may be attempts to conceal the marriage from the potentially jealous Bori spirit. There are many ancient precedents for such ideas including this from *Tobit* vii:

7:11 I have given my daughter in marriage to seven men, who died that night they came in unto her: nevertheless for the present be merry. But Tobias said, I will eat nothing here, till we agree and swear one to another.

7:12 Raguel said, Then take her from henceforth according to the manner, for thou art her cousin, and she is thine, and the merciful God give you good success in all things.

7:13 Then he called his daughter Sara, and she came to her father, and he took her by the hand, and gave her to be wife to Tobias, saying, Behold, take her after the law of Moses, and lead her away to thy father. And he blessed them;

7:14 And called Edna his wife, and took paper, and did write an instrument of covenants, and sealed it.

7:15 Then they began to eat.

7:16 After Raguel called his wife Edna, and said unto her, Sister, prepare another chamber, and bring her in thither.

7:17 Which when she had done as he had bidden her, she brought her thither: and she wept, and she received the tears of her daughter, and said unto her,

7:18 Be of good comfort, my daughter; the Lord of heaven and earth give thee joy for this thy sorrow: be of good comfort, my daughter.

8:1 And when they had supped, they brought Tobias in unto her.

8:2 And as he went, he remembered the words of Raphael, and took the ashes of the perfumes, and put the heart and the liver of the fish thereupon, and made a smoke therewith.

8:3 The which smell when the evil spirit had smelled, he fled into the utmost parts of Egypt, and the angel bound him.

8:4 And after that they were both shut in together, Tobias rose out of the bed, and said, Sister, arise, and let us pray that God would have pity on us.

8:5 Then began Tobias to say, Blessed art thou, O God of our fathers, and blessed is thy holy and glorious name for ever; let the heavens bless thee, and all thy creatures.

8:6 Thou madest Adam, and gavest him Eve his wife for an helper and stay: of them came mankind: thou hast said, It is not good that man should be alone; let us make unto him an aid like unto himself.

Figure 3: The *Akh* or Crested Ibis from tombs at Beni Hassan. The picture shows its supposed 'luminous' plumage that was thought to be a key to the word's meaning although modern research suggests the word is derived from the bird's characteristic call.[12]

8:7 And now, O Lord, I take not this my sister for lust but uprightly: therefore mercifully ordain that we may become aged together.

8:8 And she said with him, Amen.

When things go wrong, Bori cults have an array of similar techniques to rectify things. These include ecstatic 'demon' dancing to pacify troublesome Bori spirits. In these Bori cults people are 'ridden by the Bori' much as Zar dancers are ridden.

Many Bori spirits are associated with disease and illness. Thus there is a Bori of Old Age (*Mallam Tsofo*). Dancing with the disease entity 'innoculates' the dancer from that disease. Hence Tremearne's use of the term 'Ban', which in its oldest sense means to consecrate, bind, curse.

Blood is the food of the gods

It is difficult to underestimate the value of food in our relationship with the kind of spiritual entities discussed above, indeed in all our dealings with the divine realm. As I revealed in the *Bull of Ombos*, blood and flesh, real and symbolic, are primary tools of Egyptian magick. So not surprisingly we discover that when spiritual entities remain unfed or are otherwise neglected they search for blood and become troublesome. This naturally leads us back to a discussion of the equivalent entities in ancient Egypt - the Akh (plural Akhw) or undead:

The *Akhw* is a term for the transfigured dead. It is represented as the Crested Ibis, a bird that recurs elsewhere in Near Eastern mythology connected with death.

Becoming an Akh is intimately connected with the funeral cult. We meet the idea first in the Pyramid Texts, where the deceased is said to fly to heaven - which may mean the Akhw may be conceived of as birds, much as the Ba is conceived. Alternatively they might be seen as the deceased gaining the power of astral flight. In the Pyramid Texts the concept is mainly linked with rebirth and resurrection either as Ra or Osiris.[13] The most frequent occuring Egyptian offering formula begins:

Hetep de nesew asir neb djedu neter Aa neb Abdu,

and is translated:

> An offering which the king gives (to) Osiris, Lord of Djedu, great god, lord of Abydos, so that he may give a voice offering (in) bread, beer, ox, fowl, alabaster, linen, everything good and pure on which a god lives for the ka of the revered one x.[14]

This above formula was adapted for the feeding of the Akhw. The famous ceremony for Opening the Mouth was probably also brought in play in this process. The Ceremony of Opening the

Mouth is in fact a complex amalgam of several ancient rites, the core of which may actually be focussed on the construction of a fetish like image - hence the centrality of the adze in the rite. Others have argued that the ceremony is replete with imagery from the birthing process.[15]

These kind of ritual acts also make the Akh. Through these magical acts the individual Akh acquires knowledge of the entire magician's armory of spells and rites. In other words the deceased acquires magic (heka) and becomes a magician (hery hebt) - regardless of his or her previous knowledge.

It is through these magical rites, that the living enter into some kind of pact with the Akh(w). Like much Egyptian magic, the pact is actually quite a simple, freeform affair and can often be improvised. One basic requirement is that the Akhw are fed on a regular basis and certainly on the anniversary of his or her death.[16] Here is an example of a simple pact from an inscription.

> 'Oh you the living who are still upon the earth, and who shall pass by this tomb. Do you desire that the king shall favour you and you shall be in honour with the great god. Then say 'a thousand of bread, etc' for I am cunning (ikr) and an akh.' [17]

The Akhw are associated with a particular kind of artifact (see Figure 4). These may look like funerary stele but they are mainly found in houses or special cult places, almost all in the Deir el-Medina region. They are quite small objects - this example just

Figure 4: The Panacht Stele, 23cm x 15cm Ramesside (c 1305-1080bc). An example of an Akh ikher en Ra (*3ḥ ikr n Rˁ*) Stele.

23cm x 15cm found in the Ramesside workers colony (c 1305-1080BC). They are connected with ancestor worship of the Akhu. They are the ancient Egyptian equivalent of a family portrait.

The most distinctive part of the inscription is the enigmatic phrase:

Akh ikher en Ra *(3ḥ ikr n Rˁ)*

- *ikr* we might translate as 'excellent', 'skillful' or my favourite - 'The cunning spirit of Ra'. These stele contain a name to whom the object is dedicated - in this case Panakht, who is shown holding an ankh and sniffing from a blue lily. He is a private person, perhaps son of Nakhtsu.

The Blue Lily

In the illustration the deceased is shown as an Akh inhaling the aroma of a flower which turns out to be the Blue Lily (*Nymphaea caerulea*). This is a perennial herb once native to the Nile Valley & Oases, the Mediterranean, Tropical Africa, Palestine and Yemen. Its natural habitat is the ponds and canals that would be at their fullest in the season of the inundation. The image occurs in many examples of this stela, found in domestic rather than funeral contexts. What I say now supplements information given in a film called *Sacred Weeds*, which currently can be viewed on the Internet. The Blue Water Lily (*Nymphaea caerulea*) is a narcotic plant native to Egypt. It is not to be confused with the lotus (*Nelumbo nucifera*) which was introduced to Egypt by the Persians in about 700BCE, probably for decorative use but also as a staple carbohydrate.[18] Ian Shaw talks of a third native white lotus (*Nymphaea lotus*) but it is the

Blue Lily that is most often represented in for example temple pillars and is the emblematic plant of Upper Egypt.[19] Hence it has a very strong association with Seth, the Egyptian god of intoxication, chaos and confusion.

The Blue Lily is a common motif in Egyptian iconography from the time of the Pyramid Texts and before. It also regularly crops up in preserved funeral bouquets, the best known example being those found in the tomb of Tutankhamen. For the 'Atenites' who worshipped the *visible* sun, both plants could act as solar symbols - the interior of the Lily has a bright yellow areola; the ripe fruit of a mandrake, a red sun like globe. However on pectoral ornaments from Tutankhamen's tomb they are found together with a combination of solar and *lunar* emblems. Images of the gods Khonsu (Moon) and Khepra (Sun) are shown together with the Blue Lily (Moon) and the Mandrake (Sun). There may also be an androgynous theme here visible on several levels, the closed lily looks phallic until it opens into its yoni like bloom.

Spell 81 in the *Book of the Dead or Going Forth By Day* enables 'Mr X' to assuming the form of the Lily (*zešen*): 'I am this pure lily that has ascended by the sunlight and is at the Ra's nose. I spend (my) time shedding it (ie the sunlight) on Horus. I am the pure that ascended from the field.'[20]

One of the very earliest representations of its psychoactive use come from a fresco of Akhenaten now in the Staatliche Museum, Berlin. The image shows Princess Meriton, consort to Smenkara, offering him two mandrake fruits together with a bud of the narcotic

Blue Water Lily. Smenkara is shown reclining on a crutchlike staff which may indicate he is ill. The offering of plants is therefore meant as a medicament.

Within a short interval of his death, King Tutankhamen's tomb was twice robbed. The tomb robbers seem to have focussed on one thing - the 'booze'.[21] I E S Edwards estimated that the robbers had stolen 400 litres of precious liquid, much of it narcotic decoctions of the Blue Lily. The beautiful jars were uncorked and discarded, the precious liquor decanted into portable skins.[22]

The Blue Lily has a pleasant non-toxic aroma. This 'Lotus' of the Nile contain potent narcotic alkaloids in the flowers and roots,. otherwise absent from the leaves, stalks and seeds. Flowers can be eaten raw but are very bitter and best ingested in beer or wine. Ancient wine was more than 10% proof. The Ancient Egyptians also pressed the flowers to produce a concentrate for addition to wine and beer. Banqueting scenes frequently show servants topping up the revellers cups with the above 'chaser' from a special jar.

These facts are still largely unknown or ignored by Egyptologists and botanists. The initial mistake was made by the botanists accompanying Napoleon during his Egyptian invasion. The Blue Lily was wrongly identified and confused with decorative food variety of 'lotus'.

However, Egyptian medical papyri, the earliest being Papyrus Ebers correctly assert it to be a poison (*seshen - sšn*) although this was discounted by Egyptologists on advice from botanists.

Nevertheless the Egyptians knew best recognising it as a narcotic - that in moderate doses depressed the central nervous system, reducing pain and producing sleep. We can surmise that according to the dose, it can provoke and or suppress dreams. In the later case, giving the patient a break from unpleasant dreams might in itself be quite therapeutic. Dreams are the matrix on which much magick is wrought, hence if one were to be magically attacked, dreams would be the battleground.

The supposedly non-euphoric Blue Lily has in the recent past been considered as a viable alternative to Heroin. Anecdotal reports do however say that some preparations are able to produce hallucinations and vivid dreams. Too much produces stupor and even death. Harer recounts an incident in Alabama where pigs were allowed to forage recently drained swampland and died as a direct result of eating the tubers![23]

It was perhaps the ancient equivalent of Rohypnol. The Turin Erotic Papyrus shows women 'under the lotus' that is to say in a state of disinhibition, sedated even.

The Egyptians were the premier physicians of the ancient world. Their mantle eventually passed to their Greek rulers. The key source is *De Materia Medica* of Dioscorides, a Greek physician working with the Roman legions under Nero. Dioscorides prescribed a decoction of the Blue Lily to allay lecherous dreams. It is again worth pointing out the connection here between the dreams and sexuality, a line of thought that continues into modern herbal texts.

Islamic physicians translated Dioscorides and used Blue Water Lily as a sedative, expecially in heart disease. Thus, knowledge of the Blue Lily found its way into Europe via Islamic and Jewish physicians, ending up in Nicholas Culpepper's 1651 Herbal entry for the Lily. Culpepper used the root boiled in wine and water, and the decoction to be drunk. He also described a distillation from the flowers to:

> 'helpeth much to procure rest and settle the brain of frantic persons. The root restrains passing of the seed (nocturnal emissions) when one is asleep, but the frequent use thereof extinguisheth venerous actions.'

The use of Mandrake takes a similar route. For example the so-called 'Micky Finn' - is described in the *Leiden Papyrus*:

> 'When you wish to make a man sleep for two days: mandrake root, 1 ounce; water and honey, 1 ounce; henbane, 1 ounce / ivy, 1 ounce. You pound them together with a lok-measure of wine. If you wish to do it cleverly, you put four portions to each of them with a glass of wine, you moisten them from morning to evening; you clarify them, and you make them drink it; [it is] very good.'[24]

The Blue Lily blooms in the morning - but is closed by midday as is the more familiar 'morning glory'. Florists treat the Lily flowers with parafin or icewater to keep them open - which provides something of a test of whether it has been tampered with or not. If the flowers close around midday, it is a pristine specimen.

Figure 5: 20th Dynasty granite statue of Seth from restored group from Medinet Habu, near Cairo, where he is shown crowning Ramesses III. Photographed by Jacques Livet, reproduced in Philip Germond's *Egyptian Bestiary*.

In the wild, its flowers rise eighteen inches above water on peduncles - after the third day the peduncle twists and draws the closed flower beneath the water, carrying its load of pollinating insects killed by the elixir - when it matures and fruits.[25] The flower's bright blue petals and brilliant yellow centre gives it an obvious solar symbolism. Blossoming for three days is also very suggestive of other mythology. For example, it is said that when combined with Mandrake it can induce a three day sleep, which may also have been important in some mystical practices.

The ritual nature of these elixirs is further underlined by the existence of special blue lotus vessels used for its inbibition. Cups made in the form of the night blooming white lotus were for daily mundane use. The Blue Lotus cups may indicate ritual or gnostic activity. (**Figure 6**). It also gives a clue to the time of day favoured by the ancient Egyptians for magical 'symposia'. The Blue Lily blooms in the early morning, and we can link this with the psycho-geographical space - the Duat. For reasons that will become clearer in the later chapters on the archaic lunar calendar - those early twilight hours just before and after dawn were especially important in the Egyptian magical religion. The original meaning of the term Duat is precisely this time. If the ancient Egyptians ever did meditate this was such a time.

Some say there is a connection between the Blue Lily and a group of medically orientated sorcerers of the scorpion goddess Selket. Presumably, Blue Lily was used as a medicament in the treament of stings and bites, the treatment of which was a specialism within their cult. Ancient Egyptian naturalists recognised two kinds of

Figure 6: Painting (with details) of blue faience chalice, now in Florence museum. See Egyptian Ceramics provenance Tuna el-Gebel

scorpion - a harmless aquatic variety, and the more troublesome terrestrial species. Selket's most ancient association is actually with the harmless variety. It was only in Ptolemaic times that the iconography shifted closer to the venomous kind. We can see how the underlying pattern might work in terms of an affiliation with the harmless water scorpion transferring some sort of protection or 'inoculation' from its more deadly 'cousin'. There is also an interesting dialectic around the phenomenon of breath. The water scorpion has a special tube that it uses to draw breath whilst remaining submerged. This phenomenon was probably observed by Egyptian naturalists. Conversely the bite of the terrestrial scorpion is known to compromise the victim's breathing causing death by asphyxiation. The water scorpion lives on submerged vegetation, which would naturally include the basal parts of the Blue Lily. The water scorpion might even be one of the plant's pollinators.[26]

More on the Akhw

So once again we are in the domain of the eating magick described in the *Bull of Ombos*. If the feeding is neglected, the Akhw become troublesome. The evolution of the concept indicates a pattern: 'The blessed or beatified state of the deceased, the potent dead, evolving into a general meaning of spirits.' Eventually these same Akhw become the dangerous undead. By the Coptic period this word has morphed to the *Secherou* -- demons. The vampiric[27] aspect of the Akhw come to the fore as they sojourn either in heaven (with Ra) or the underworld (with Osiris).

All of this brings us into the domain of another popular

phenomenon, *Letters to the Dead*.[28] The recipient of such a letter can be a deceased relative or a complete stranger. The living writers of such letters have a sense of being afflicted by a malign entity. As this is seen as coming from the realm of the dead it seems natural to enlist a dead relative to sort it out. To do this the deceased must be 'cunning' enough to act on your behalf.

"Then become an akh for me [before] my eyes that I may see you fighting on my behalf in a dream.'

Letter to the Dead [29]

In ancient Egypt there was a reciprocal relationship between the living and the dead that was part of an extremely popular ancestor cult. Sometimes the ancient Egyptian rejected or grew tired of this relationship. In those circumstances, the undead became a problem. It is also the reason why there is a similarity between these Letters to the Dead and another group of texts known as 'Execration texts'. This really does bring us squarely into the domain of Seth, the model for all such activities. An Old Kingdom pot of the time of Pepi II, found in the Giza necropolis relates to this issue. The jar has holes for suspension or binding, encircling the object with cord - a quintessential technique of Egyptian magick.[30]

All this suggests techniques that are still quite viable in a modern context. There are several ways in which we might interact with these ideas, for instance to frame a recently, or not so recently departed relative, as an otherworld ally. Secondly to respond to the unwanted attentions of the undead Akhw. Thirdly there are undoubtedly some who might wish to take on this role - either after death, or perhaps even whilst still enjoying this life. They might want to become Akhw whilst still living. The realm of influence for all these activities is the world of dreams.

To establish a dead relative as a Akhw you need:

1. An image of a dead relative

2. A pact

3. Regular feeding - the most common offering would be bread and beer. In ancient Egypt we can surmise that the beer was to be flavoured with red ochre - which would give it a slightly metalic blood-like taste. It reminds us that the ultimate food of the gods was flesh and blood. This is a very old theme whose latest form is found in the eucharist, but may originally have been some ritual cannibalism of a kind described in the *Bull of Ombos*. The drinking of blood by the Akhw is one reason Egyptologists routinely refer to them as Vampires.

4. Write them letters.

5. Special days

There were probably special feast days on which to placate the Akhw. Perhaps Wag - strangely omited from various *Almanacs of Lucky and Unlucky Days*, although other fitting days to placate the Akhw are mentioned in the almanac[31] (see chapter 1.4). More detailed information on appropriate days for this type of activity will be discussed below, in connection with ancient Egyptian archaic lunar calendar.

To drive away the Akhw

To deter the unwanted attentions of the Akhw, especially those perceived in the dream world one needs:

1. To know their name and form - perhaps via divination.

2. An execration rite to get rid of them.

To become Akhw

There are four principal points of entry:

1. Divine intervention.

2. Assumption of an appropriate god form - there are several to choose from, principally the sun-god Ra, the creator Atum, Osiris or my own favourite Seth.

The Book of the Dead or Going Forth by Day has several spells for 'entering the mind of a god' with this intention. This book seems to me to be a collection of quite diverse magical material. The simpliest way to accomplish this would be to paint an image, ideally a hieroglyph of the appropriate god, on a piece of papyrus using red oche ('Nubian pigment'). Recite the spell over this, and make offerings of food, especially blood and incense on the appropriate days, ie the new moon, the sixth day feast, *Wag*, *Thoth*, the god's birthday etc. Details on how to calculate these days will occupy my later chapters. The scroll is then worn around the neck as a discrete amulet.[32] It entitled the wearer to travel in the barque of Ra along with other *Akhw*.

Notes:
1. Neugebauer O & Parker, R (1962) *Ancient Egyptian Astronomical Texts*, 4 vols, Brown University.

2. A history of night-time in western society before the Industrial Revolution, between the late Middle Ages and the early nineteenth century. See also O'Dea, WT (1958) *The Social History of Lighting*, London. Rossotti, Hazel (1993) *Fire*, Oxford.

3. To 'fight evil with evil' has an interesting parallel with ancient medicine, see for example - katharsis - whereby state of equipoise is achieved by encounters with extremes. Consider also homeopathic and allopathic modes. The best example of a surviving ancient medical system is to be found in Indian's Ayurvedic (science of longevity) medicine. The aim in this is also some form of kathartic balance. Although this system developed in India, it contains many international concepts - such as those which were common currency in the ancient near east, including Egypt.

4. Szpalowsja, Kasia (2003) *Behind Closed Eyes: Dreams & Nightmares in Ancient Egypt*, Wales. The author argues that Egyptian dreams - reset (*res.t*) literally 'to awaken', has no verbal form. Ie a dream is something one sees rather than does. On the other hand 'sleep' is a verbal noun, hence in Demotic one encounters 'evil sleep' netket bin (*ntkt bn*)

5. Gardiner, Sir Alan and J Cerny (1957) *Hieratic Ostraca*, Oxford. HO109

6. Ritner, Robert (1990) 'Ostracon Gardiner 363 - a spell against night terrors.' *JARCE* 27 25-41.

   DNdet mʿnmty pn n ḥr-imy-snw.t

   'Fortress of Horus etc' - I think Nemty might also be a reference to the underworld ferryman Nemty - a form of Seth, who as ferryman has various roles warding off the ultimate demon Apep/Apophis]

7. Ritner, R *op cit*
8. Assmann J, ÄHG (Ägyptische Hymnen und Gebete) No147.
9. Baines, J. (1989) ed with K Schousbue, *Literacy and Society*, Copenhage.
10. Mercer, S A B (1949) *The Religion of Ancient Egypt*, London, London, Luzac 1949).: 45
11. Tremearne, A J N (1914, 1968) *The Ban of the Bori: Demons and Demon Dancing in West & North Africa*, Cass.
12. Lepsius C R (1849-59) *Denkmaeler aus Aegypten und Aethiopien*, 12 vols, Prussia. Janák, Jiøí (2006) 'New light on the Akh-bird', *Current Research in Egyptology* 2006
13. For Ra see PT 990a & 152 a-d; Osiris PT 899a, 1487c, 633a, 1637a etc.
14. Collier, M & Bill Manley (1998 : 35) *How to Read Egyptian Hieroglyphs,* BM Press. BM EA 558.
15. Smith, Mark The Ceremony of Opening the Mouth for Breathing; Budge, Wallis, The Book of Opening the Mouth for Breathing; Roth
16. Demarée, Robert J. (1983) *The 3ḫ ikr n Rᶜ Stelae. On Ancestor Worship in Ancient Egypt*, Leiden. : fn83
17. Demarée op cit : 212. Urk I 218.7 - 219.7
18. Emboden, William (1989) 'The Sacred Journey in Dynastic Egypt: Shamanistic Trance in the Context of the Narcotic Water Lily and the Mandrake, *Journal of Psychoactive Drugs* Vol 21(I) Jan-Mar pp 61-75 : 65
19. Shaw, Ian & Paul Nicholson (1995) *The Dictionary of Ancient Egypt*, BM
20. Allen, T G (1974) *The Book of the Dead or Going Forth By Day*, Chicago. I made some amendments. The vignette that accompanies this spell shows a blue lily rather than a lotus. The ancient Egyptian equivalent of 'Mr X' is N or NN.

21. 'Booze' is an Egyptian word for homebrewed alcohol of a type still widely drunk throughout Africa.

22. Edwards 1972 *Treasures of Tutankhamun*, BM section 3 'Floral Unguent Vase'.

23. Harer W Benson (1985) 'Pharmacological and Biological Properties of the Egyptian Lotus' Hayes, JARCE XXII pp49-54

24. PDM xiv 727-36 Griffith and Thompson, *The Leyden Papyrus* p.149 1.XXIV/17-26. Revised translation by Janet J Johnson in Betz 1986.

25. Emboden *op cit*

26. Encyclopedia of Ancient Egypt, Oxford. Entry under 'Medicine' . Ghalioungui, Paul *The Physicians of Ancient Egypt*. [357 Gha (fol)]; Frédérique von Känel (1983) *Les Prêtres-ouâb de Sekhmet et les conjurateurs de Serket*, BEHE 87 [357 Kan]; Lexicon 'Selqet'; Sauneron, Serge ( ) Le Papyrus Magie de Brooklyn [383.4 sau]; Un Traité Égyptien d'ophiologie, papyrus du Brooklyn Museum [383.4 sau fol]

27. Meeks D, (1971) Génies, anges, et démons en Égypte' in Génies, Anges and Démons, Sources Orientales VIII, Paris.

28. Demarée 1983 : 213

29. Demarée, 1983 : 216

30. Osing, J (1976) MDAIK 32 p133-185. The use of the term ah ikr is difficult to explain here.

31. The days are: II Akhet 14; II Akhet 17; IV Akhet 30; I Peret 9; II Peret 4; II Peret 7; II Peret 28; IV Peret 28; IV Shemu 19. This won't mean much without reference to my later chapters of Renpet, the 'wheel of the year.' and the lunar calendar of Ancient Egypt.

32. Allen, T G *op cit* Spells 144 T(erminal rubric) 1 - 7 and Spell 148 P(relimimary rubric) 1

2. An Egyptian Origin for the European Vampire Myth

The magick discussed in the previous chapter is not unknown in the modern world, although it might well appear under a different name such as creating a 'thought form' or 'servitor'. Thought forms and servitors can make interesting experiments, but anecdotal accounts show how they can also become troublesome; the most common problem being their refusal to go away. There is a well known story that comes from the 'psychic questing' circles, which tells of how they cooked up an entity called, let's say 'John', who was a fictional ghost, whose purpose was merely to be an illustration or paradigm in lectures on ghost hunting. But pretty soon 'John' began turning up outside of the lecture hall and in the end become such a nuisance that he had to be banished.

'John' may have been a troublesome creation because he was so banal. If to begin with, he had had a more interesting 'biography' perhaps the results would have been less troublesome. As I recalled in my book *Tankhem*, the psychic experiments of the poet W B Yeats with his wife 'Georgie' had very contrived beginnings but took on a very significant life of their own. There are many lessons to be learnt here concerning the relationship between the liminal and 'real' worlds.[1]

An Egyptian origin for the European Vampire myth

'Vampire' comes from the south Slavic word *Vampir*. Hence we tend to associate vampires with Slavic culture. That is to say 'one of the revenant undead found in Slavic folklore. These are categories of social undesirables, such as murderers, thieves, whores, heretics and witches, who may become vampires, leaving their coffins at midnight to have *sex with the living, or feed off their blood* (my emphasis). A sharp stake of hawthorn or aspen might be driven through the corpse as a means of ensuring that the dead would rest in peace. Elsewhere, corpses might be *beheaded, dismembered or mutilated*. In Croatia, ankles and heels were maimed to prevent the dead from walking.'[2]

The preceeding passage brings to mind the Ostraca spell discussed in chapter one, which also utilises the technique of bodily reversal to prevent possession by these morbid ancestral spirits. The head turned backward was also described in more detail in *The Bull of Ombos*.

Undead creatures such as Egyptian Akhw occur all over the Ancient Near East and Mediterranean. For example: 'The Lamia of ancient Greece and the Roman striges or mormos were ghosts with similar characteristics; they returned from their burial place, usually in bodily form, but sometimes, as Ovid asserts, as *fierce birds* (my emphasis), to visit humans by night and devour them or drink their blood. The lamia was generally portrayed as a beautiful woman who would lure an unsuspecting, rosy-cheeked youth into her clutches and then devour him. This illustrates another principle of vampires, particularly female vampires; they are traditionally thought to be insatiably amorous and sensual.'[3]

In the Indian subcontinent these creatures are called the Dakini or Yogini. The worship of them lies at the heart of Tantrism - but that's another story.

The 'vampiric kiss' is a prominent theme in Egyptian medical texts. It has the power to inflict a stroke on the victim or sexually inject their bodies with a 'hostile influence' (Aaa - 𓄿𓄿). One example from the Brooklyn Magical Papyrus describes a ritual to protect the owner during sleep against being raped by a demon via the ear!

'Witchcraft'[4] also existed in ancient Egypt, but it was feared not nearly as much as the vampiric kiss of the Akhw - the undead. In fact the Egyptian tendency to attribute illness and misfortune to the agency of demons and ghosts stands in marked contrast to other societies' emphasis upon human witchcraft.'[5]

Rituals for dealing with this kind of spirit possession have survived into the present day via the Zar cults of Egypt, Ethiopia and Sudan. The eminent anthropologist Enno Littmann studied the cult's oral tradition which records an Egyptian origin. A 'priestess' in this tradition is called a 'Shecha' a word derived from Coptic Secherou and Egyptian 'Akhw'. Jan Fries, in his book *Seidways* translated and made available some of Littmann's research:

'In ancient times a sultan of the spirits fell in love with the daughter of the Pharaoh and through the mouth of a wise priest he asked to marry her. But the Pharaoh did not permit it. Full of rage, the spirit sultan entered the body of his beloved, and made his home within her. Soon the Pharaoh's daughter became very ill. Her face turned pale and her will to live waned. For weeks she just dozed on her bed, weak and sad, in the twilight realm between life and death. Seeing his daughter suffer, the Pharaoh sent for healers, seers and sorcerers. Many wise men came to the court, some with rare elixirs, others with spells and exorcisms, but the spirit sultan was stronger than any of them. From day to day the princess became weaker, from day to day the messengers of the Pharaoh searched the country, until at long last they met an old healer at the very limits of Upper Egypt, her name was Zara. She was the daughter of a priest and a good friend of the spirits. Making great haste, the messengers brought Zara to the court. Here, Zara took the appropriate measures. First, she smoke-bathed the obsessed princess thoroughly. Then she prayed, and asked the spirit-sultan to appear, and to speak with her through the mouth of the princess.

'Welcome', old Zara said to the spirit-sultan. 'What is your wish?' . . .

'I came into the body of this princess as the Pharaoh has refused to let her be my wife. I like it this way, and now, my spirit relations have seen it, they want to come and obsess all the ladies of the court. But you have come and interfered. You came and asked me what I wish. For you, Zara, only for you will I leave the body of this princess, provided you hold a night-feast in my honour.'

'We will be glad to do so', said Zara, 'what sort of feast do you want?'

The spirit-sultan replied: 'set up a table for the sacrifice. Light candles for me. Slaughter animals, chant, play on drums in this style (and he showed her the proper words), and I will leave the princess. She will return to better health than before.'

It is the Zar spirits who, speaking through the mouth of the patient, specify which remedies and offerings will heal the disease. These remedies are often sacrificial gifts for the spirits, or talismanic jewellery for the patient, or simply blood.

The Zar spirits can be of any gender. A person obsessed by a Zar spirit will be treated like the spirit. A woman obsessed by a male spirit will be addressed and treated like a man, and a man obsessed by a female Zar will be dressed up and treated as a woman. This is undoubtedly not easy for many Islamic men, which may indicate why relatively few men join the Zar cult. 'Ridden', a word that brings Voodoo to mind, is also used to designate Zar obsession. Zar devotees are refered to as 'yazâr faras' which means 'Horse of the Zar'.

Abyssinian Christians know the Zar as descendants of Cain. Another interesting tradition are the words chanted during the rite. A good many of them lost their meaning centuries ago, such as the chorus-words

'wedawâ-wedeh; wâdéh wâdéh; wadaiya; ayaway wâiyéh'.[6]

If a bit of demon dancing doesn't sort out troublesome spirits, then more drastic measure were and are called for. Those spirits that are now too vampiric have to be punished by the use of some very effective but unpleasant measure.

Those that would feed on us are themselves to be eaten. Their hearts are extracted (vampires have no heart) and they are given as food to the gods.

Thus the line in the Ostraca spell from chapter one:

> 'Your heart is destined for the sacrificial meal of the cobra goddess.'[7]

This sacrificial meal is no mere jest. Such sacrificial meals did occur at one of the most famous festivals in the ancient world - that of Letopolis (khete khawy - *ḫ - t - ḫ3wy*).

Letopolis, the 'City of Leto' ; Egyptian name Khem, modern name Ausim is just north of Cairo. It was the capital of second Egyptian nome whose titulary deity was the falcon god Khenty-Irty (a blind form of Horus) also known as Khenty-Khem - 'Foremost of Khem'. It is a place that has strong associations with ancient stellar magick. It is mentioned several times in the so-called *Cairo Calendar*, a proto-astrological text, which I prefer to call an *Almanac of Lucky & Unlucky Days*.

Letopolis is a place to be called to mind whenever one has 'Typhonian' demons that need to be cooked and eaten. On the face of it, Letopolis appears to be a stronghold of Horus, the principal adversary of Seth. But are things quite that simple? Perhaps the Rekhyt - the folk know something we don't?

Very little remains of Letopolis, but it is obviously one of those places that was in *very* early times actually a stronghold of Seth. Perhaps he held this position jointly with his brother Horus. The nome standard or 'Totem' of Khem is the Khapesh or Bull's Leg or in later times the constellation of the Great Bear. As I argue in my book the *Bull of Ombos*, this constellation is a symbolic representation of Seth. The four stars that form the 'enclosure' of the constellation the Great Bear, are also called the Four Sons of Horus.[8]

Letopolis presents us with further evidence as a possible focus for ancient cannibalistic rites. The spell's threat to eat trouble-some ancestors recalls some of the possibly cannibalistic funeral rites discussed in the *Bull of Ombos*. The Sethian way of death may well contain elements designed to deter the evil dead.

Letopolis owes its existence to a special natural phenomenon - connected with meteorites. Letopolis is one of several such 'thunderbolt cities'.[9] There is also a strong association between meteorites and oracular dreams. They may even have played a role in their deliberate incubation. The Egyptian word for meteorite - Biat (*Bi3t*) - is the same as for iron and not surprisingly becomes a new word for 'oracle' or 'wonder'.

Thunderbolts, meteorites and 'arrows from heaven' should all remind us of Seth. Seth is sometimes shown with an arrowlike tail and in a relief of Tuthmosis III he guides the king's arrow as he shoots at his Sed festival.

Later, during the time of the Ramessides, the consultation of oracles became very popular. The gods were said to express their will directly to the plaintiff via oracles.[10]

Some people speculate that there was a time in the second millenia BCE, when the number of meteorites hitting the earth was much higher than it is today. Could this be an explanation for the preponderance of thunderbolt mythology all over this region? When scholars looked at the local geology of Letopolis, especially the incidence of fossils, they found another possible explanation of the thunderbolt imagery. In the ancient world, fossils were often connected with thunderbolts and meteorites. And indeed there, the large 'thunderbolt' fossil *(Nerinea Requieniana)* is very common in the area and unknown elsewhere.

The Letopolitan worship was clearly very ancient, and when it was attempted to assimilate the original god Khenty Irty (*ḥnty-irty*) to the myth of Horus and Seth, the result was very ambiguous. Hnty-Irty nominally became Horus of Letopolis, yet he and his city have much to do with Seth.[11]

Jacob's Ladder

In the Old Testament's account of 'Jacob's ladder' - we read that Jacob slept with a meteorite for a pillow and as a consequence, enjoyed a visionary dream of angels ascending and descending a heavenly ladder:

'Taking one of the stones of the place, he put it under his head and lay down to sleep. And he dreamed that there was a ladder set up on the earth, and the top of it reached to heaven; and behold, the angels of God were ascending and descending on it!. . . So Jacob rose early in the morning, and he took the stone which he had put under his head and set it up for a pillar and poured oil on top of it. He called the name of that place Bethel; but the name of the city was Luz at the first.'[12]

Such a dream might also be had in Letopolis. It was a place of ascent with its own ladder, or 'stairway to heaven', constructed from

Figure 7: Images of Seth in canid form with strange arrow-like tail.

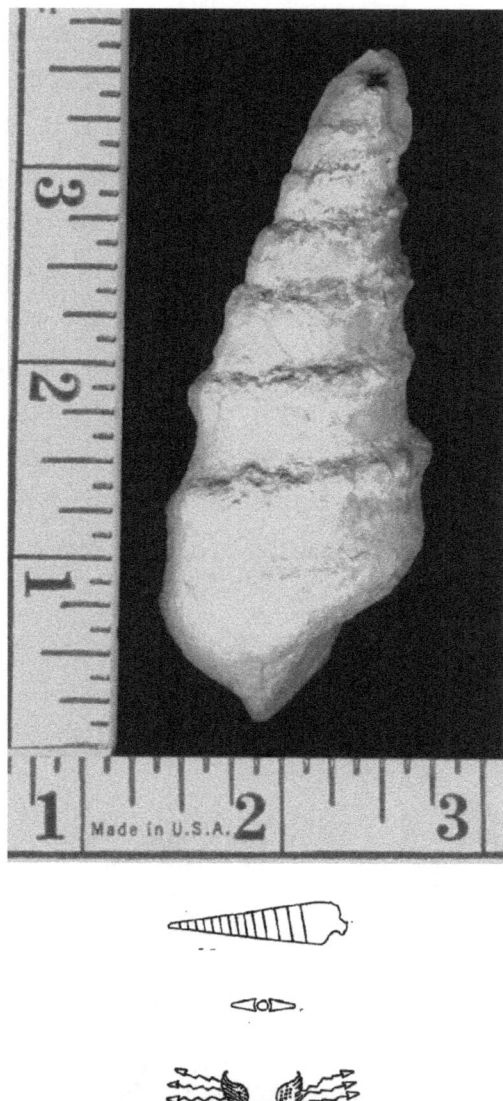

Figure 8: *Nerinea DeFrance* similar but smaller than *Nerinea Requieniana*. Detail shows drawing of fossil alongside the thunderbolt or 'fishtail knife' symbol of Letopolis together with a classical image of the thunderbolt from Gerald Wainwright's article.

or held up by Seth or sometimes Horus and Seth. Here it was thought especially likely that the justified could ascend to the imperishable stars. It was also a place where ones inner motives were tested to destruction.

So what happened at the Festival of Letopolis? The celebrated Egyptologist and folklorist Gerald Averay Wainwright speculated that the rites involved some form of fire walking, whereby one was literally tested in the flames just as happened to Shadrach, Meshach and Abednego in the Old Testament *Book of Daniel*.

Those that fail the test the future is bleak - cooked and offered up as food to the city's cannibalistic inhabitants especially Horus the Elder, a cannibal especially fond of blood. Interestingly Horus the Elder is often viewed as the origin of the vampire myth. Which incidentally is another example of eating and cannibalistic magick discussed in the *Bull of Ozabos*. It also shows that Seth, who is usually seen as the one who controls and sends the demons and vampires to do his bidding, is also involved in the process of their disposal! Thus in Egyptian religion, no 'evil' is absolute.

Notes

1. For more information on troublesome spirits see

    Letter Pap Leyden I 371, Gardiner-Sethe 'Letters to the Dead' pp8-9; G Posener (1981) 'Les afarit dans l'ancienne Egypte' *MDAIK* 37 pp393-401; J F Boughouts 'The annoyances of a revenant' in *CdeE* forthcoming; Gardiner Later Egyptian Stories 'Khemsemhab & the Spirit'

2. Bently, Peter, (1996) *The Hutchinson Dictionary of World Myth*, pp. 217-218.

3. Jones, Alison (1996) *Larousse Dictionary of World Folklore*, 444-5

4. Edwards I ES (1960) *Hieratic Papyri In the British Museum, 4th series - Amuletic Decrees*, BM. 'Witch' would be *hekau* with feminine determinative.

5. Ritner, Robert (1990) 'Ostracon Gardiner 363 - a spell against night terrors.' *JARCE* 27 25-41 : 34

6. See Chapter 'Horse of the Zar' in Jan Fries (1996) *Seidways: shaking, swaying and serpent mysteries*, Mandrake, Oxford. Other sources: Leiris, Michel (1958) *La Possession et ses aspects théatraux chez les Ethiopiens de Gondar*, Paris;. Lewis, I M (1971) *Ecstatic Religion*, Penguin books; Messing, Simon (1958) 'Group therapy and social status in the Zar cult of Ethiopia' *American Anthropologist* 60 pp 1120-7; Littmann, Enno (1950) *Arabische Geisterbeschwörungen aus Ägypten*, Harrassowitz Verlag, Leipzig. A J N Tremearne (1914) *Ban of the Bori: demons and demon dancing in West and North Africa*. Hossan Ramzy, Rhythms of the Nile CD.

7. Ritner, Robert (1990) *op cit*

8. Wainwright, Gerald Averay (1932) *Letopolis, JEA 19* pp. 164-167. In the pyramid texts the four children and their father (*hnty-irty*) of these the first group take up its position on the 'side of T which is in Horus, while *hnty-irty* joins Seth's wife Nephthys on the other side 'which is in Seth.' Pyr ¶601

9. Wainwright, Gerald Averay (1932) *op cit*

10. Assmann, Jan (2001) *The Search for God in Ancient Egypt*, translated by David Lorton, Cornell.

11. Wainwright, Gerald Averay (1932) *op cit*

12. Genesis 29 : 12-22

3. Egyptian Psychology

So far we have been looking at a cluster of related magical spells that together make an operational chain.[1] In this chapter, we consider the ways in which ancient Egyptians analysed dreams in search of malign or non-malign characteristics. This will bring us into the domain of ancient Egyptian psychology.

In some respects the modern practitioner might well look at it in much the same way as the ancient Egyptian. Back then there were two principal techniques used to analyse dreams for possibly curses. First, by the use of manuals of dream interpretation; second, by use of *Almanacs of Lucky & Unlucky Days*. The later, as we shall see, is related to very ancient, that to say pre-Greek, but proto-Egyptian 'astrology'.

The Egyptians were famous in the ancient world for their ability to interpret dreams. Just think of the Biblical story of Joseph and his bumpy career as an interpretor of dreams, during the supposed 'captivity' of the ancient Hebrews in Egypt.[2]

The Egyptians made use of manuals of dream interpretation. The oldest surviving example comes from a collection of hieratic manuscripts in the British Museum, edited by Alan Gardiner.[3] Most people might think that ancient Babylon would be the natural home of this kind of thing. But as it happens, the oldest extant example is from Egypt rather than Mesopotamia. This manuscript is 19th dynasty (i.e. c1400BCE Ramesside) but is widely believed to be even older with 12th dynasty antecedents (c2000-1750BCE). Gardiner tells us that 'these [dream manuals] are [still] popular throughout the less educated classes in the western world,' - which is presumably you or I.[4]

You might think that a bad dream is a fairly obvious thing - but looking at the dream manuals, this is far from being the case. Some dreams are subject to 'ironic reversals'.[5] For example a dream of death or a funeral could be a good omen - the very fact of having a funeral was seen as a good thing by the Egyptians - it signified an orderly departure - besides there's the question of that inheritance! There is also a fondness for puns (paronomasia) and sexual situations:

If a man sees himself in a dream his penis becoming large.[6]

This is a good omen meaning his possessions will multiply.

Interpretation relied as much upon analysing the nature of the *dreamer* as the dream. Compare this with Sigmund Freud, *The Interpretation of Dreams*, where one needs to know something about the dreamer before interpretation is possible. If you look through my transcription of the dream manual at the end of this chapter, a definite personality type emerges.

I quoted Jacob Dielemann elsewhere as saying that 'During the later stages of the pharaonic religion, Seth's role had become restricted to representing the archetypical enemy of the ordered world.' The further you go back, the less restricted is Seth's role - until you arrive at a very ancient time, then he was one of the most important of Egyptian gods. Even so, these dreams manuals show that in the popular psyche - Horus and Seth ruled supreme, as they did at the beginning and as they continued to do until the end of Egypt and beyond. The compilers of this dream manual thought it essential to list the good and bad dreams of both kind of man - Horians and Sethians. Both kinds of people were capable of good and bad dreams.

The dreams of women

From the surviving manual, we learn of two personality types - those who are followers of Horus, and those who are Typhonians. But it is also clear that these are the dreams of men. From examining a related material, I strongly believe that there would be a corresponding manual for the dreams of women. Although, a women's dream manual has not so far been discovered, we can surmise that they would also fall into two broad personality types - those of Isis and Nephthys, the divine counterparts of Horus & Seth.

In my opinion, the Egyptians thought that anyone could have either, Horus & Seth; Isis & Nephthys within them, like Yin / Yang, animus/anima etc. Yes, certain people, perhaps certain ethnicities or racial types, could be predominantly one or the other. But any one person could in the appropriate circumstances manifest Seth or Horus. Or, to use an Egyptian idiom: 'the god in him is Horus'; 'the god in him is Seth'; 'the goddess in her is Isis'; 'the goddess in her is Nephthys'.

Egyptian personalities
The god in him is Horus

> O Horus (*khenty-irty*) of Letopolis. It is repeated anew. Mighty of strength, master of fear, save me from bad and evil things and from any slaughter. Horus, son of Geb
>
> Spell to be said on the birthday of Horus
>
> (see Chapter 1.4)

The beginning of the source manuscript is damaged and lacks the general definition of the Horus personality type, but we can surmise how this would be. The Horian is more 'patrician', in contrast to the more plebian (rekheyt). This term *rekheyt* is interesting. The Egyptologist Alan Gardiner thought it might be yet another reference to the Companions of Seth?[7]

Apart from its introduction, the Horus section is less damaged and list many more distinctive dreams. This was further subdivided into good dreams - listed first, followed by a selection of malefic dreams.

The manual contains an incantation spell, similar to the one above to defend against evil sleep. Its presence here shows the connection between dream manuals and defence against such episodes. Alan Gardiner also felt that this is a 'hint that Horus was regarded as the prototype of the normal Egyptian man whose nocturnal visions were interpreted in the first half of the book. The text of the spells is unhappily rather corrupt, though not to the extent of rendering it wholly unintelligible. The form of a dialogue is adopted, Horus calling upon his mother Isis to shield him from the baneful consequences portended by his dreams. These consequences are of course ascribed to the machinations of Seth.' I am not so sure. given that the final Typhonian section is missing and might indeed have contained their corresponding spell of protection.

> (10, 10) to be recited by a man when he wakes in his (own) place.
> ' "Come to me, come to me, my mother Isis.
> Behold, I am seeing what is far from me in my city."
> "Here am I, my son Horus, come out with what thou hast seen, in order that thy afflictions(?) throughout thy dreams may vanish, and fire go forth against him that frighteneth thee. Behold, I am come that I may see thee and drive forth thy ills and extirpate all that is filthy."
> "Hail to thee, thou good dream which art seen <by> night (10, 15) or by day. Driven forth are all evil filthy things which Seth, the son of Nut, has made. (Even as) Ra is vindicated against his enemies, (so) I am vindicated against my enemies."
> <u>This spell is to be spoken</u> by a man when he wakes in his own place, there having been given to him pesen-bread[8] in (his) presence and some fresh herbs moistened with beer and myrrh. A man's face is to be rubbed therewith, and all evil dreams that [he] has seen are driven away.'

The god in him is Seth

> Son of Nut, great of strength ...... protection is at thy hands of thy holiness. I am the son of thy son.
>
> Spell to be said on the birthday of Nephthys
>
> (see Chapter 2.1)

Being a batchelor was seen as a very Sethian thing.

Being drunk was another and incidentally the Egyptians didn't see drunkenness as a wholly bad thing - drunkenness was for them an important way of communicating with the divine. See *Almanac of Lucky & Unlucky Days* discussed at length in a later chapter. Those born on certain days are predicted to suffer death by drunkenness although this is no bad thing:

> Month II, day 6 : f. f. f. A happy day for Ra in heaven, and the gods are pacified in his presence. The Ennead is making glorification in front of the Lord of the Universe. Anyone born on this day will die in a state of drunkenness.
>
> *Almanac of Lucky & Unlucky Days*

The Typhonian section follows, preserving a general introduction to the Typhonian type. This character analysis is (so far) unique in Egyptian writings. It is followed by the listing of good dreams. A final section on the malign dreams of the Typhonians is missing, but we can presume it would have included a defensive spell similar to that of the Horians.

This section confirms the official dislike for Typhonians, either because they have red hair or for some other reason were believed to be adherents of Seth. The destiny of the Typhonian is subject to different laws'.[9]

From this text we learn something of the distinguishing marks (literally brands - Ab - *3b*) of the followers of Seth. This begins with an indication of physical stature but the unit is missing. Longevity is given for various situations in one instance 84 years - but falling to sixty if the Sethian remains unmarried.

The ideal Egyptian life expectancy was 100 even 110 years, although the average in the Ptolemaic period was actually 54 for men, 58 for women, but could be even less depending on social class.

> If the god in him is Seth, then he is a man of the people (rekheyt).

Then follows various fragmentary descriptions of his red hair colour and features. Then a possible allusion to his being accident prone.

> 'He is one dissolute or discontent of heart on the day of judgement. Discontent in his heart.'

Heart is here used in the concrete sense as the seat of consciousness and organ assessed in the famous Judgement scene of Spell 125 of the *Book of the Dead or Going Forth By Day*.

Then some recommendations. I.e Sethians shouldn't drink. 'If he drinks a beer, he drinks it to engender strife and turmoil. The redness of the white of his eye is this god. He is one who drinks what he detests.'

> He is beloved of women through the greatness of his loving them. He likes women and consequently they like him.
>
> Though he is a royal kinsman, he has the personality of a man of the people (Rekhyt).

That word for the folk used again. In some ways, all this could be a sketch of the famous King Ramesses II - who was a red head and may well have lived into his one hundredth year.

'... he would not descend unto the west, but is placed in the desert as a prey to rapacious birds ...'

As for a man who is a drunk, (who) broils, (causes) calumnies, ills and mischief. He drinks beer so as to engender turmoil and disputes . . . he will take up weapons of warfare . . . before him, a hippopotamus ... when he perceives on the second day (Gardiner suggests when he wakes up after a drinking bout - which is amusing but more likely to be a reference to a festival) . . . he will not distinguish the married woman from ... as to any man who opposed him ... massacres arise in him and he is pleased in the Netherworld. . . He will engender disputes so as to break vessels' - the rest is too fragmentary to make much sense of, but you get the idea.

The goddess in her is Isis

'Thou hast thy blood, O Isis
thou hast thy magical power'
The Book of the Dead or Going Forth by Day[10]

Isis or Aset (*3st*) was the principal role model for ancient Egyptian women. She is the goddess of love in its socially acceptable form. Jan Assmann sums her up as the representative of the lifegiving power that stems from romantic attachment. The more unacceptable forms would fall to her rival Hathor. Hathor is a goddess with a much older pedigree. Her cult can be traced back to a neolithic cattle cult. Isis appropriates many of Hathor's attributes but in the process makes them more civilized and less 'savage'. Even so, despite Isis representing wifely love and devoted motherhood, she can be ruthless in pursuit of these ends - hence her relentless pursuit of her husband (Osiris's body) and her sometimes deadly anguish to those, often innocent interlopers who find themselves in the wrong place at the wrong time. For example, according to Plutarch, the King and Queen of Byblos assisted Isis in recovering the body of Osiris. The subsequent lamentations of Isis were so loud and terrible that they killed the younger of their sons. She then took the second of their young sons back with her to Egypt, only to lay upon him such a terrible look that he too died of fright.[11] She can also be contrary, finding compassion for her 'savage' brother Seth in his moment of weakness.

The so-called Knot of Isis is one important emblems. The Knot of Isis represents her blood and magical power. This is a female version of the famous Ankh sign - and in both cases is probably some form of garment covering the generative parts and hence its meaning of 'life'. We can thus conclude that it refers to a healthy, fecund woman in the prime of her life.

In mythology Isis has a crucial function in the cult of divine kingship, where she is the goddess of physical restoration which she accomplished by the magical power of speech. She is one of the mourners and sustainers of the deceased, hence one of the four guardians of the canopic jars.

Figure 9: Symbol of the Rekhyt, the folk or conquered people. According to Alan Gardiner perhaps also designating the Sethian or Typhonian or 'underdogs'. The image often appears in temples and may indicate areas open to the common folk. The image is based on the lapwing - which fakes injury in order to decoy potential predators from its nest - hence its contemporary use as a symbol of a secret tradition within witchcraft.

The goddess in her is Nephthys

Oh, Nephthys, daughter of Nut, sister of Seth, she whose father sees a healthy daughter, beautiful of face. Beautiful of face.* I am the divine power in the womb of my mother Nut.

Spell to be said on the birthday of Nephthys
(see Chapter 2.1)

Nephthys is a sister, the introverted sister and counterpart of extrovert Isis. She is much more a representive of the dark, saturnine personality, so although in cult of divine kingship she shares many crucial functions with her sister Isis, she would be associated with the descending night boat of Ra, whereas Isis stands in the ascending day boat. She personifies selfless help to others, often in the form of healing, mothering and nursing. She has important functions in association with birth but more as midwife than actual mother.

She is the sister and wife of Seth, and this an awareness of her former alliances is always in the background. Even so, she is never hostile to Osiris and according to Plutarch, bears him a son, Anubis. In reality she represents the archetype of the childless women - by reason of her extreme youth or age derived lack of fertility. The ancient Egyptians probably had a different attitude to childlessness than elsewhere in the ancient world. They were certainly more favourably inclined towards adoption.

She is rarely seen apart from her sister Isis, with who she sings the famous lamentations to the stricken Osiris. She has thus changed

---

*   In several ancient languages duplication is used to add emphasis.

sides and this desertion may be part of the motivation for Seth's murderous rage against his brother Osiris. She is also one of the mourners and sustainers of the deceased, and as such can represent death and decay.

Her name means 'housewife' and this 'tamed' nature is reflected in her hieroglyph which shows the groundplan of a house with a symbol for mistress which also looks like a cleaning bowl.

Mercer says she is sometimes called lady of the west, also associated with the goddess of fate and also the headless goddess of the west called 'justice'.[12]

Unlike Isis, there is far less cultic material on Nepythys although there is evidence of a small priesthood. She features heavily in the Pyramid Texts, for example the *Cannibal Hymn*. This later text alludes to an otherwise unknown piece of her mythology, whereby she is said to lack a vagina but is otherwise very beautiful. The only other reference to her in Old Kingdom literature is the *Memphite Theology*.[13]

Although a shadowy presence in official literature, she may well have had a more lively existence in the popular magical tradition of the folk (Rekhyt). She is featured in the Ramessium Papyri - found in a magician's box along with several other interesting artifacts. From this, we can surmise that she has a hidden magical side as the Red Goddess - more closely aligned to Seth. And indeed the *Greek Magical Papyri* contains at least three rare but extremely interesting invocations of Nephthys in her more Sethian mode. The example below is fairly revealing of her character type as maid and crone:

Apollonius of Tyana's old serving woman:
Take Typhon's skull [Ass] and write the following characters on it with the blood of a black dog:

"⌷ ⚵ ⌓ ☉ ⌔ ⚹ SABERRA"

Then, going to a suitable place, by a river, the sea, or at the fork of a road, in the middle of the night put the skull / on the ground, place it [under] your left foot, and speak as follows:

The formula: "ERITHYIA MEROPÊ GERGIRÔ CHÊTHIRA ANAPEROUCH . . .LYRÔPHIA GÊGETHIRA LOLYN GOUGÔGÊ AMBRACHA BI... AEBILÊ MARITHAIA MPROUCHE ABÊL ETHIRAÔ AP... ÔCHORIÊLA MÔRÊTHIRA PHECHIRÔ ÔSRI PHOIRA AMERI... PHÊ. OUTHÊRA / GARGERGIÔ TITHEMYMÊ MÊRAPSÊCHIR AÔRIL.

Come, appear, O goddess called Mistress of the House. (Nephthys)"

After you say this, you will behold sitting on an ass a woman of extraordinary loveliness, possessing a heavenly beauty, indescribably fair and youthful. As soon as you see her, make obeisance and say: "I thank [you], lady for appearing to me. Judge me worthy of you. May your Majesty be well disposed to me. And accomplish whatever task I impose on you."

The goddess will reply to you, "What do you have in mind?"

You say, "I have need [of you] for domestic service."

At that, she will get off the ass, shed her beauty, and will be an old woman. And the old woman will say to you, "I will serve and attend you."

After she tells you this, the goddess will again put on her own beauty, which she had just taken off, / and she will ask to be released.

But you say to the goddess, "No, lady! I will use you until I get her."

As soon as the goddess hears this, she will go up to the old lady, and will take her molar tooth and a tooth from the ass and give both to you; and after that it will be impossible for the old woman to leave you, unless perhaps you want to release her. From that time forth, you will receive a bounty of great benefits, for everything that your soul desires will be accomplished by her. She will guard all your possessions / and in particular will find out for you whatever anyone is thinking about you.

Indeed, she will tell you everything and will never desert you: such is her store of good will toward you. But if ever you wish, there is a way to release her (but never do this!). Take her tooth and the ass's tooth, / make a bonfire, and throw them into the fire, and with a shriek the old woman will flee without a trace. Do not be prone to release her, since it will be impossible for you to replace her.

But do release the goddess, when you are sure that the old woman will serve you, by speaking as follows: "menerpher phie prachera lylori / melichare nechira." When the old woman hears this, the goddess will mount the ass and depart. *The phylactery to be used throughout the rite:* The skull of the ass.

Fasten the ass's tooth with silver and the old lady's tooth with gold, and wear them always; for if you do this, it will be impossible for / the old woman to leave you. The rite has been tested.[14]

The above concludes this short excursion in ancient Egyptian dream lore amongst whose function was prognostication concerning a person's fate as determined by factors at their birth, their personality type and whether they are prone to demonic attack from divine or human agencies.

The mysteries of the 'dreamy night air' were especially appropriate for the god Seth, who had many associations with dream control. Dream control of one sort or another was a common element of ancient magick. In the next chapter we look at some ancient methods to protect against the terrors of the night. In the appendix to this chapter you will find the surviving parts, including blank pages, of the ancient dream manual. You are invited to complete these with your own observations.

Notes

1. Chaîne Opératoire in modern anthropological jargon (see glossary).
2. Assmann, Jan (1997) *Moses the Egyptian*, Harvard.
3. Gardiner, A H (1935), *Hieratic Papyri in the British Museum (HPIBM) series III* vol 1 text.
4. Gardiner 1935: 22
5. Ritner, R K (1996) 'Dream Oracles' in Hallo, William W, *The Context of Scripture* Vol I, Brill.: 52
6. 2.11 (Horus section) see Gardiner 1935

7. See Gardiner 1935 (Typhonian Section II.1 - footnote) for supposition that this word signifies Confederates of Seth.

8. Pesen = flat round bread rather like Pitta.

9. Gardiner 1935: 9

10. Spell 156. The book's title is peret em herew (*prt m hrw*) - 'Book of Going Forth by Day' although more commonly known to us as The Book of the Dead. Allen, T G (1974) *The Book of the Dead or Going Forth By Day*, Chicago.

11. Plutarch, Isis & Osiris, XV, translation by

12. Muller, *Mythology* 52-3, 100

13. The sometimes rather grandly termed *Denkmal Memphitischer Theologie* being the text found on the Shabaka Stone now in the British Museum. Allen, J P (2000) *Middle Egyptian: an introduction to the language and culture of the hieroglyphs,* Cambridge. This text alone, is enough to place Egyptian thought squarely in the line, at the beginning of western philosophy. (p173).

14. PGM XIa 1-40 translated by Hubert Martin, Jr. in Betz (1986). For other rare invocations of Nephthys, see PDM xiv 1219-27 Nephthys as a healer (as opposed to Isis's role as maker of magick -- and fevers caused by seizure of the south wind; PDM LXI 100-105 The Red cloth of Nephthys.

Appendix: Ancient Egyptian Dream Manual

Table: 1.1 The Dreams of the Followers of Horus 1.00			
If a man sees himself in a dream			Most of the first section is damaged and mostly lost. Luckily the next page is far more extensive. But judging by what remains of this page it would have contained a personality profile of the Horus man. The number of dreams lost is unknown. I include some of the fragmentary interpretations for the light they still shed on the personality type.
		good	
		good	
		good	it means putting . . . in his hand

Table: 1.2 The Dreams of the Followers of Horus 2,00			
If a man sees himself in a dream	with his mouth split open	good	it means something he was afraid of will be opened up by the god.
	eating the fruit of the carob	good	gaining authority over his townsfolk
	a crane	good	it means prosperity.
	honey with its top covered	good	it means the [gift] of something to him by the god.
	his townsfolk circulating around him	good	
	Eating lotus leaves	good	something he will enjoy.
	shooting at a target	good	something good will happen.
	given a blade	good	something to make him happy.
	[mentioning?] his wife to a husband	good	it means the retirement of ills that were besetting [him].
		good	
	his penis becoming large	good	it means his possessions will multiply.
	.... a bow in [his] hand	good	his important office will be given to him.
	dying violently	good	it means living after his father.
	seeing the god who is above	good	it means much food.
	seeing a serpent	good	it means food.
	.... has entered [into] his	good	it means annihilation of words.
	[drinking] .... beer	good	it means his heart overflows.
		good	much food will come to him.
	reducing (his)	good	it means the reduction of his(?)
	his mouth full of earth	good	eating (the possessions of) his townsfolk.
	eating donkey-flesh	good	it means his promotion.
	eating crocodile flesh	good	[it means] eating the possessions of an official.
	up a growing tree	good	it means his loss of.........
	looking out of a window	good	the hearing of his cry by his god.
	rushes being given to him	good	it means the hearing of his cry.
	seeing himself on a roof	good	it means finding something.

Table: 1.3 The Dreams of the Followers of Horus 3, 0

If a man sees himself in a dream	a pond	good	it means a road will collapse for him.
	seeing himself [in] mourning	good	the increase of his possessions.
	his hair becoming long	good	it means something at which his face will brighten up.
	white bread being given to him		
		good	it means something at which his face will brighten up.
	drinking wine		
		good	it means living in righteousness.
	sailing downstream,	good	tying his ......
	copulating with his mother	good	clansmen will cleave fast to him.
	copulating with his sister		
		good	it means the bequeathing of something to him.
	up a dum-palm	good	it means joy at what his inclination has prompted.
	seeing long fingers	good	it means the entrusting of something to him by his god.
	people beating him with blows	good	it means something . . . to him.
	seeing a ...... with him	good	establishing his . . . in his heart.
	seeing (mn) a dead ox	good	it means seeing {mtt} [the death?] of his enemies
	seeing	good	his . . . overthrown.
	a man [having been sent to him]	good	great . . . His . . . a great mission.
	a woman		
		good	against a woman by [her?] husband.
	a head being given to him	good	opening his mouth to speak.
	being purified	good	
	binding fast a donkey	good	
	upon a large pedestal	good	
	going forth [upon] earth with a leg	good	
	being given a magic flail	good	
		good	
	copulating with ?	good	
		good	

Table: 1.4 The Dreams of the Followers of Horus 4, 0			
	killing (smim) a snake	good	killing (smim) words.
	seeing his face as (that of) a leopard	good	acting as a chief.
	seeing a large cat		it means a large harvest will come to [him].
	drinking wine		opening his mouth to speak.
	binding fast baleful men by night		taking away his enemies' utterance.
	crossing in a ferry-boat		it means an issue from all words.
	seating himself upon a tree		the destruction of all his ills.
	killing an ox		killing his enemies.
	sightseeing in Busiris		having a great old age.
	fermenting(?) dates		it means finding victuals.
	climbing up a mast		his being suspended aloft by his god.
If a man sees himself in a dream	destroying his clothes		his release from all ills.
	seeing himself dead		a long life [in] front of him.
	binding fast his own legs		it means sitting among his townsfolk.
	falling from a wall		it means an issue from words.
	carving up an ox with his (own) hand		killing his (own) adversary.
	fetching vessels out of the water		finding increased life in his house.
	seeing herbs of the field		finding meals for his father.
	picking dates		it means finding victuals given by his god.
	cultivating spelt in the field	good	
	being given victuals belonging to a temple		the bestowing of life upon him by his god.
	sailing in a boat		it means sitting among his townsfolk
	picking bones		finding a meal [from] the royal palace.
	flax in the field		
	river		the hearing of his cry by his god.
	the hearing of his cry by his god		

Table: 1.5 The Dreams of the Followers of Horus 5, 0 -

If a man sees himself in a dream	flax in the field	good	
	river	good	the hearing of his cry by his god.
	[drinking?] blood	good	putting an end to his enemies.
	[drinking] milk	good	a large meal will come to him.
	drink[ing] his (own) urine		eating his son's possessions.
	silver and gold	good	a large meal from the royal palace.
	knocking a stone against his finger	good	it means the giving to him of his cattle.
	[hewing?] stone	good	it means the giving of something to him.
	reading aloud from a papyrus	good	the establishment of a man in his house.
	carving up a female hippopotamus	good	a large meal from the royal palace.
	crocodile[s]	good	it means acting as an official.
	[eating] donkey	good	eating a meal [from] the royal palace.
	sitting in an orchard in the sun	good	it means pleasure.
	dislodging a wall	good	it means absolution from ills.
	[eating] excrement	good	eating his possessions in his house.
	having connection with a cow	good	passing a happy day in his house.
	eating crocodile [flesh]	good	[acting as] an official among his people.
	directing (a jet of) water	good	prosperity.
	plunging in the river	good	it means absolution from all ills.
	spending the night upon the ground	good	eating his possessions.
	seeing carobs	good	finding a good life.
	[seeing] the moon shining	good	pardoning of him by his god.
	veiling himself	good	the removal of his enemies from his presence.
	falling(?)	good	it means prosperity.
	sawing wood	good	his enemies are dead.

Table: 1.6 The Dreams of the Followers of Horus 6, 0 -

If a man sees himself in a dream	burying an old man	good	it means prosperity.
	cultivating herbs	good	it means finding victuals.
	bringing in the cattle	good	the assembling of people for him by his god.
	working stone in his house	good	the establishment of a man in his house.
	throwing his clothes upon the ground	good	it means the issue from words.
	towing a boat	good	his landing happily in his house.
	threshing grain upon the threshing floor	good	the giving of life to him in his house.
	eating grapes	good	the giving to him of his own things.
	planting gourds	good	the giving to him of a good life through the gift of his god.
	writing on a column	good	seeing his life to be good.
	burying something alive	good	it means prosperity (and) life.
	breaking into [a boat] that has foundered	good	the giving to him of his wife.
	binding fast	good	the giving to him of his house later on.
	seeing a princely blossom	good	prosperity.
	capturing [a female] slave?	good	it means something from [which] he will have satisfaction.
	eating	good	food will come to him.
	munching	good	something will come (into) his possession.
	seeing barley and spelt [given?]	good	it means the protection of him by his yonder god.
	seeing himself weak	good	it means a man's finding enemies dead.
	there being given to him beads		prosperity.
	praising	good	his being found innocent before his god.
	a gift	good	it means equipping his house with something.
	a living tomb upon earth	good	it means his possessions will become large.
	seeing Beduins	good	the love of his father when he dies will come into his presence.
	seeing himself with one greater	good	it means his promotion by his (own) agency.

Table: 1.7 The Dreams of the Followers of Horus - Bad 7, 0 -

If a man sees himself in a dream	entering into the temple of a female	bad	
	eating notched sycamore figs	bad	it means pangs.
	copulating with a female jerboa	bad	the passing of a judgement against him.
	drinking warm beer	bad	it means suffering will come upon him.
	eating ox-flesh	good	it means something will accrue to him.
	munching a cucumber	bad	it means words will arise with him on his being met.
	walking on a	bad	it means the starting upon words with him.
	eating a narr-fish that has been split	bad	his being caught by a crocodile.
	munching (dsis)	bad	it means hostility (dsis).
	removing one of his legs	bad	judgement upon him by those yonder.
	seeing his face in a mirror	bad	it means another wife.
	the god making his tears cease	bad	it means fighting.
	he seeing himself with a pain in one side	bad	the exaction of something from him.
	eating hot meat	bad	it means his not being found innocent.
	shod with white sandals	bad	it means roaming the earth.
	eating what he detests	bad	it means a man's eating what he detests.
	copulating with a woman	bad	it means mourning.
	he being bitten by a dog	bad	a cleaving fast to him of magic.
	being bitten by a snake	bad	it means the arising of words with him.
	measuring barley	bad	it means the arising of words with him.
	writing on a papyrus	bad	the reckoning up of his misdeeds by his god.
	stirring up his house	bad	[it means] his falling ill.
	having a spell put upon his mouth by another	bad	it means mourning.
	acting as steersman in a ship	bad	in any judgement of him he will not be found innocent.
	his bed catching fire	bad	it means driving away his wife.
	waving a rag	bad	it means his being mocked.
	pricking himself through a thorn	bad	it means telling lies.
	seeing the taking of birds	bad	it means the taking of his possessions.

Table: 1.8 The Dreams of the Followers of Horus - bad 8, 0 -

	seeing his penis stiff	bad	stiff victory to his enemies.
	sailing downstream	bad	it means a life of bitterness.
	being given a harp	bad	it means something through which he fares ill.
	looking into a deep well	bad	his being put in prison.
	he catching fire	bad	he will be massacred.
	removing the nails of his fingers	bad	removal of the work of his hands.
	filling pots	bad	it means his having pangs.
	folding wings around himself	bad	he will not be found innocent with his god.
	copulating with a kite	bad	it means robbing him of something.
	seeing an ostrich	bad	harm befalling him.
	his teeth falling out	bad	it means a man's dying through his dependents.
If a man sees himself in a dream	seeing a dwarf	bad	the taking away of half of his life.
	fallen a prey to the council	bad	his being driven from his office.
	being beaten with a stick of willow	bad	it means the absence of mourning when he dies.
	entering into a room with his clothes wet	bad	it means fighting.
	shaving his lower parts	bad	it means mourning.
	splitting stone	bad	it means his god is discontented with him.
	melting down copper	bad	it means roaming the earth.
	feeding cattle	bad	it means roaming the earth.
	shutting up his house	bad	it means a rebuff.
	snaring birds	bad	it means being deprived of his possessions.
	notching a tree	bad	it means depressing ailments attacking him.
	building his house	bad	the fomenting of words with him.
	carrying off property belonging to a temple	bad	the removal of his possessions in his presence.
	putting incense [upon] the fire to a god	bad	the might of a god against him.
	throwing wood into the water	bad	the bringing of pain into his house.

Table: 1.9 The Dreams of the Followers of Horus - bad 9, 0 -

If a man sees himself in a dream	putting a seat in his boat	bad	it means putting away his wife.
	being made into an official	bad	death is close at hand.
	an Asiatic garment upon him	bad	his removal from his office.
	seeing people afar off	bad	his death is at hand.
	eating an egg	bad	the seizure of his possessions beyond repair..
	smearing himself with fat	bad	the taking away of his people from him.
	attaching a chariot	bad	words have suddenly arisen against his person.
	seeing the heavens raining	bad	words have come up against him.
	seeing a woman's extremity	bad	the last extremity of misery upon him.
	uncovering his own rearend	bad	he will end an orphan later.
	eating figs and grapes	bad	it means illness.
	pressing out wine	bad	pressure on his possessions..
	plastering his house with Nubian ochre	bad	it means the removal of his people.
	putting his face to the ground	bad	the requirement of something from him by those yonder.
	seeing a burning fire	bad	the removal of his son or his brother.
	copulating with a pig	bad	being deprived of his possessions
	sitting in the hull of a boat	bad	the dragging of his own heart.
	drinking blood	bad	a fight awaits him.
	cutting his hair	bad	the removal of something from his house.
	seeing his face in the water	bad	making free with another life.
	weaving the thread of a loincloth	bad	the taking away of his possessions.
	copulating with his wife in daylight	bad	the seeing of his misdeeds by his god.
	brewing beer in his house	bad	it means being turned away from his house.
	pounding barley and spelt	bad	the requirement of what he has
	building himself a house	bad	harassing words await him.
	seizing wood belonging to the god	bad	finding misdeeds in him by his god.
	looking after monkeys	bad	a change awaits him.
	fetching mice from the field	bad	a sore heart.
	sailing downstream	bad	violent words.
	eating faience	bad	strong words.
	making a festal chamber	bad	the bringing to light of his misdeeds.
	tending small kids	bad	the perishing of his possessions.

Table: 1.10 The Dreams of the Followers of Horus - bad 10, 0 -		
measuring barley with the corn-measure	bad	his victuals overflow
eating ox-flesh	bad	a boxing fight
quenching (fire) with water	bad	the end of his possessions
putting beer into a vessel	bad	the removal of something from his house
breaking a pot with his feet	bad	conflict
The Horus section finishes here with the incantation against evil sleep and then begins the Typhonian section with a physical and psychological profile.		

If a man sees himself in a dream

Table: 1.11 The Dreams of the Followers of Seth - Good 11, 0 -			
If a man sees himself in a dream	being given a goat carved up into [its] good members	good	
	standing on a height of the earth with a sceptre in his hand	good	
	walking in a pen for goats	good	
	throwing rushes into the water	good	
		good	it means something with which he will be elated
	The remainder is too fragmentary to translate or missing		

1.4 Lucky or Unlucky?

'They assign each month and each day to some god; they can tell what fortune and what end and what disposition a man shall have according to the day of his birth'

Herodotus II.4 82

Fate, karma, luck, all of these might play some role in whether you are vulnerable to supernatural assault. Some people may well by more vulnerable by reason of their birth. The ancient Egyptian certainly thought so and their approach laid down the basis of the astrology as perfected by the Babylonians and Greeks. In this chapter, I will discuss two principal sources - *Almanacs of Lucky and Unlucky Days* that seem to have been put to use as some kind of guide to the natal 'horoscope'. The second related documents are so-called *Amuletic Decrees,* which are in effect a more detailed statement on the perils that menace the future life of the new born Egyptian.

Before the emergence of the familiar twelve signs of the zodiac, ancient Egyptians had a system of Decanal astrology. The Decans are thirty-six deities each of whom presides over ten degrees of the celestial horizon or decanal belt. The Stele of Merneptah relates how in 13th century BCE Egypt, it was widely accepted that there was a close connection between constellations and historical events here on earth, especially war.[1]

The Decan system seems to be a product of the First Intermediate

Period circa 2125-1975BCE. Decans first appearing on coffins then in more monumental contexts such as the astronomical monuments of Vizier Senmut. Late versions of the Decans are depicted as snake-form deities - some with lionid heads and others with wings. It is a remarkable change in iconography. Decans also begin to appear on amulets and bracelets, this custom spreading outside of Egypt, appearing for example on a 6th century plaque from Carthage.

The Decans are the protectors and emissaries of Hathor, sometimes her frightful executioners. They also have a strong association with Hippo - another aspect of fate. Decans often appear on Egyptian ritual jewelry - The Museum of Fine Arts, Budapest, has an example of a golden necklace laced with thirty-six miniature hippos.[2] Decans also occur on the 'menit' - an amulet or perhaps counterpoise symbolic of the goddess Hathor, but also worn by gods Ptah and Khonsu. The Menit bears the aegis of Hathor/Bast as mistress of the Decans. As an hieroglyph the menit (*mnit*) is used to write words connected with suffering and malady.[3]

Many of these artifacts are made of cheap materials and it is therefore safe to assume a popular usage.

The were also some established associations, noticeable in magical texts, between certain Decans and for example the Osirian family see for example Sejet (*sj.t*) 'The sheep'. Decanal lore is part of Egypt's proto-astrology, that is one of components of the planetary astrology of later times. Perhaps fear of meteorites, which

Figure 10: Menit showing gods of the Decans in various registers. Staatliche Museum, Berlin. See citation in footnote 1

emanating from various Decans, gave rise to this and other omens so prominent in the times of Ramesses the Great.

Amuletic Degrees

These are narrow six centimetre wide strips of papyrus taken from the end of the roll. In style, these are specialised forms of private letter. You may recall I mentioned the importance of 'Letters to the Dead' in Chapter 1.1. These were rolled up into a tiny scroll with the owner's name on the outside. This was then tied with thread and deposited in an amulet (see Figure 11 & 12) and worn as a charm. Their provenance is largely unknown but seems to be Thebes. Their usefulness ends with death of the owner but may have been included with personal effects in the tomb. One example mentions the name of 21st dynasty Prince Osorkon - which places them anytime 929BCE to 730BCE.

They are called *decrees* because a god is prognosticating to a third person on behalf of a child. A blank is left in the text for activating word 'Djed (*dd*) - said'. The contents of these amulets are focussed on this life not the next, which demonstrates how the ancient Egyptians were not as obsessed with the afterlife as some commentators would have us believe. These Amuletic Decrees reflects the growth of *personal piety*, which as we discussed above became prominent at the time of Ramesses II. From this time on, 'god' expresses his or her will directly to the person via phenomena such as oracles and decrees. The most celebrated oracles of this period begin their existence outside of the temple, although they are later brought inside or appropriated by the priesthood. The special term for oracle is BiAt (*Bi3t*) the same word designates

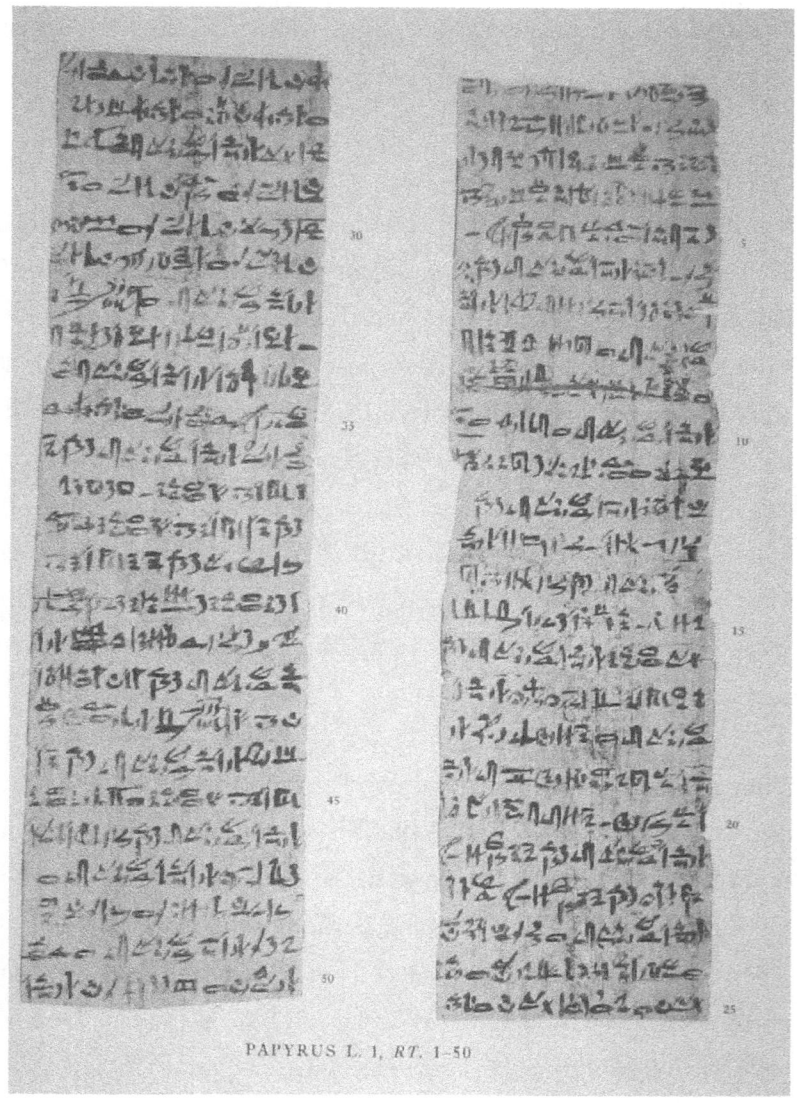

Figure 11: Papyrus text of an amuletic decree. This to be rolled up and placed in an amulet holder an example of which is shown in Figure 12.

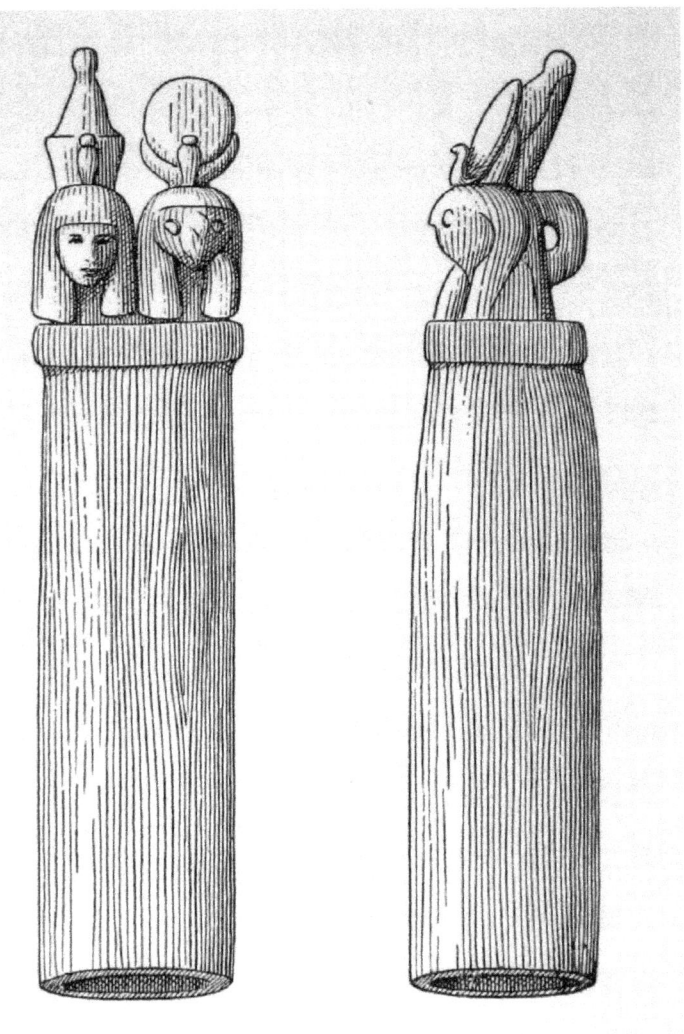

Figure 12: Wooden container for Amuletic Decree P4. The original was discarded after this drawing was made.

meteoric iron. The etymology is perhaps an indication that oracles are linked to meteorites and the quadrant of the sky from which they fell. The Amuletic Decrees often mention fear of the seven stars meaning Ursa Major, a constellation mostly associated with the god Seth. Four stars of this constellation form a box, and were called the Four Sons of Horus. This is evidence of an earlier affiliation as the Four Sons with Seth (see material in previous chapter on Letopolis). One of the most famous oracular festivals was that of Opet at Luxor (see later chapters below).[4]

These amulets are often responses to oracles and were utilized for the benefit of newborns of either sex. Edwards studied seven male examples and fourteen female. The parents take on the role of sponsor - termed a Bak (*b3k*) - literally a servant or perhaps in this context a devotee. The decrees contain very few expressions of rank which suggests they are for the common people - the Rekhyt. Amuletic Decrees provide yet another window onto the life of the ordinary person - providing in passing many small details such as the fact that children played minor sacerdotal roles such as 'sistrum player of Mut'.[5]

The major purpose of the Amuletic Decree is to provide immunity from disease, successful reproduction in adulthood with a promise of male and female offspring. They also desire their offspring to be protected against accidents, stings and bites. The parents wishes are for modest prosperity which is seen in the above simple values rather than some glittering career.

Here is a fairly typical example

Amuletic Decree L1
(British Museum 10083)[6]

I. Khonsu-who-was-a-Child and Khonsu-the contriver (pairsekheru), those two great living baboons who rest on the right and left of Khonsu in Thebes Neferhotep[7] and who are those who issue a book of death and Life. We shall keep her safe from Sekhmet and her son [Miusis rather than Nefertem].

We shall keep her safe from the collapse of a wall and from the fall of a thunderbolt.

We shall keep her safe from leprosy, from blindness, and from the eyes of the undead (?) throughout (her) whole lifetime.

We shall keep her safe from the seven stars of the Great Bear and we shall keep her safe from the star which falls from the sky and strikes one down. We shall keep her safe from the Ennead of the Upper Egyptian On; we shall keep her safe from their abominations; we shall cause them to be content because of her and cause them to answer her prayers.

We shall keep her safe from the *Books of the beginning of the year* and from the *Books of the end of the year*.

We shall keep her safe from every (kind of) death, from every (kind of) illness, from every (kind of) accusation, from every (kind of) wrong, from every (kind of) disorder, from every (kind of) frustration (?), from every (kind of) unpleasant word, from every (kind of) harsh word, from every (kind of) mean word, and from every (kind of) mockery.

We shall keep her safe from every evil, from every evil eye, from every evil glance (?), from every evil injury (?), and from every evil colour.

We shall keep her safe from the manifestations of Amun, Mut, Khons, Mont, and Maat.⁸

We shall keep her safe from a harsh oracle and a harsh word.

We shall keep her safe from the gods who seize someone in flight (?), from the gods who seize someone by capture (?), from the gods who (40) find someone in the country and kill him in the town or *vice versa*.

We shall keep her safe from every god and every goddess who assume manifestations when they are not appeased.

We shall keep her safe from the gods who seize someone instead of someone (else).

We shall keep her safe from the Great Noble in Heliopolis.

We shall keep her safe from every action of a *hayty-demon* and from every action of a *shmay-demon*.

We shall keep her safe from every malady and from every fever.

We shall cause strength to flourish in every limb of hers.

We shall keep her safe from every god and every goddess of the entire land, in heaven, on earth, in the South, in the North, in the West, and in the East.

We shall keep her safe from a wrecking of the heart and from a sinking of the heart.

We shall open her mouth to speak. We shall keep her from harm on every kind of pilgrimage which she may make, in every sanctuary (?) which she may enter, and in every place to which she may go.

We shall guard her at midday, we shall keep watch (over) her at night, and we shall take care of her by night, by day and at (all) times.

We shall keep her safe from the gods of the decans who return to their fellow gods.

We shall keep her safe from every evil Semay *(sm3y)-demon* and We shall keep her safe from any bad confusion (?) in speech.

We shall keep her safe (on) (board) ship, on the desert-edge, and on any kind of journey which she may make in (?) any place she wishes.

We shall provide everything that is good for her, every... that is good and a happy childhood.

We shall keep healthy her hands and their ten fingers.

We shall keep healthy her sides.

We shall keep healthy her abdomen.

We shall keep healthy her *pudenda*.

We shall keep healthy her rectum.

We shall keep healthy her entire abdomen.

We shall keep healthy her thighs and her shins.

We shall keep healthy her ten toes.

We shall keep healthy her body and all her limbs from her head to the soles of her feet.[9]

Mont-Re-Harakhty, lord of Thebes, who is residing in the Upper

Egyptian On, [said]—Inyt, who is residing in the Upper Egyptian On, these great gods, the eldest who were the first to come-into-existence,

[said]:

'We shall keep safe our servant and our offspring'

NN whose mother is NN.

We shall keep her safe from demons of a canal, from a demon of a well, from a demon of a river, from a demon of a lake, from a demon of (a pool) left (by the inundation), from a male demon and from a female demon, from a demon of her father and her mother and from a demon of the relatives of her father and the relatives of her mother.

We shall propitiate them for her and we shall preserve her from them throughout her whole lifetime. We shall keep her safe from the magic of a Syrian, from the magic of a Nubian, from the magic of a Libyan, from the magic of the people of Egypt, from the magic of a warlock and a witch and from all magic of every kind.

[. . .]

We shall keep her safe from any internal ailment and any sickness which has (ever) happened.

We shall bring Amun to her at his time.

We shall not (allow) anyone to stand up before her.

We shall bring Nekhbet to her when she is propitiated.

Thus said (they), namely the great gods, the eldest who were the first to come-into-existence: "As regards every good thing which has been included in this oracle as well as those (things) the inclusion of which has been forgotten," they are like those (things) which are placed before us daily, we shall make them beneficial (to) our servant NN, whose mother is NN-khons.

We shall (cause her) to conceive male children and female children, we shall cause her to let (them) go forth, we shall cause (her) to send them away and they will report back to her.

We shall provide her estate with cattle, with goat(s), with male-servants and female servants, with barley, with emmer, with copper and with apparel.

Almanac of Lucky and Unlucky Days

A study of the sources that went into the composition of the festival calendar at Esna has revealed a New Kingdom literary text. The later is a unique 'calendar' or more properly an *Almanac of Lucky and Unlucky Days* that mentions goddesses of every day of the year as well as related 'abominations'.[10] The manuscript date to 19th dynasty times of the Ramesside kings. It is more accurately called an *almanac* than a true calendar although, the difficulties of interpreting the dates of the ancient Egyptian festival year have led many, erroneously in my opinion, to interpret it as such. There are, however, no readily visible relationship between these lists and those otherwise consulted for the study of festivals in for the classical work of Siegfried Schott.[11] The terms Heb 'festival' and Peret 'going forth' as used in the Cairo 'calendar' may represent simple forms of celebration of the god, if any specific ritual expression is involved at all.[12]

The extant myths are not background to ritual but real and present events bringing with them good and bad days. They are a descriptions of the immediate world as seen from the perspective of the inner rooms of the temple. Their popularity is open to debate, for example records of the workers village at Deir-el Medina, show no indication that the prohibition on workdays was ever observed.[13]

The reader need only turn to my later chapters for a comprehensive guide to the actual Egyptian lunar and solar year. The information given is essential if you want to try and coordinate the prognostications of these Almanacs with real dates.

The Cairo 'calendar' presents several mythological episodes embedded in the text. It is assumed that myths selected for inclusion must have had some privileged status. Dominant amongst them, as we might expect, are myths of the Sun God Ra. For example, in the entry for I Akhet 22 (ie 22 day of the first month of the inundation) Ra eats the other gods. Next in prominence are myths of Nun, the cosmic waters, upon whom the boat of Ra sails forth. His power is said to be such that the earth trembles under him (III Akhet 4).

The Cairo 'calendar' abound in episodes that bode potential danger; incidents such as the 'Legends of the Eye' and other angry goddesses; their retrieval and passification. There is several mentions of the going forth of the divine emissaries or executioners, much feared by the ancient Egyptians.[14] You will recognise many legends connected with the burial of Osiris and naturally enough for an almanac that deals with lucky and unlucky days, legends connected with the conflict of Horus & Seth. For example, we learn some things about the power of Seth's voice (III Peret 5); its ability to cause dissention, and the ability of speech to defeat him (II Akhet 2). We also find repeated episodes from other famous texts such the transformation of Horus and Seth into Hippopotami (I Akhet 26).

Predictions, prohibitions and ritual behaviour

The Almanac presents us with information on: The origin of the cosmos, gods, mankind and animals; The world of the dead and transformations; ritual or magical practices; The idea of destiny; Festivals; Prohibitions and taboos; ethics. So for example there are forty days on which the almanac recommends staying indoors; seven days where death by old age is predicted for the new born. We also read prediction of death by drunkenness was considered a reasonable death for the ancient Egyptian.

Each month begins with the phrase: 'House of Re, House of Horus, House of Osiris' - the significance of which is obscure but perhaps underlines the fact that this is more of an almanac than a true calendar.

The transition between the old and new year is a moment fraught with particular danger. This reminds me of the 'dangerous twilights' of the Hindu tradition. This furnished with special apotropiac spells of which several versions are known. The full text of these spells to Osiris, Horus, Seth, Isis and Nephthys is given in my chapter 2.1.

Lucky, Lucky, Lucky

Depending on which version of the almanac one consults, the day is said to have either two or three parts.[14]

This the first column of the almanac has either the hieroglyph:

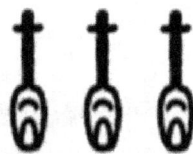

NFR, NFR, NFR –

(F)ORTUNATE, F. F.

or

'h', 'h', 'h' –

(A)DVERSE, A. A.

Hence some days can be one part favourable, two parts unfavourable.

The first and last days of each month are always lucky, the only exception to this rule is II Peret (Harvest) 30.

The 20th day is invariably adverse.

The 10th day is always favourable in Akhet (Inundation); in the archaic lunar calendar to be discussed in a later chapter, the 10th would fall at the beginning of the 'white nights' of the moon's middle phase. This day is always adverse in Peret (Winter) and alternative adverse and favourable in Shemw (Harvest).

Appendix I: Almanac of Lucky & Unlucky Days

AN INTRODUCTION TO THE BEGINNING OF INFINITY AND THE END OF ETERNITY which the gods and goddesses of the shrine and the assembly of the Ennead HAVE MADE (AND) WHICH THE MAJESTY of HAS GATHERED TOGETHER in the great house in the presence of the Lord of the Universe. WHAT HAS BEEN FOUND IN THE LIBRARY IN THE REAR-HOUSE OF THE ENNEAD.

HOUSE of Ra (Tomorrow)

HOUSE of Osiris (Yesterday)

HOUSE of Horus (Today)

AKHET: INUNDATION SEASON FIRST MONTH:

DAY 1: F. F. F. The birth of Ra-Harakhte; ablution throughout the entire land in the water of the beginning of the High Nile which comes forth as fresh Nun, so they say. And so, all gods and goddesses are in great festivity on this day, and everybody likewise.

DAY 2: F. F. F. If you see anything [in the sky], it will be good on this day. It is the day of the going out of the Ennead before Ra, their hearts being pleased when they see his youthfulness (after) they had killed him who rebelled against their master, and overthrown *Apophis* wherever he might be who fell on his back amidst the flood.

DAY 3: F. F. A. Anyone born on this day will die by a crocodile. It is the day of making *ipy* in the river by (?) the gods of the Duat.

DAY 4: F. F. A. Do not do anything on it this day. It is the day of the going forth by Hathor together with the executioners (flowercutters) in order to approach the river-bank. Now the gods go in a contrary wind. Do not navigate in a boat on this day.

DAY 6: F. F. F. If you see anything, it will be good on this day (it will be good). The gods are peaceful in heaven at navigating the great barque.

DAY 6: A. A. F. Anyone born on this day will die of the trampling of a bull.

DAY 7: F. F. F. It is the day of welcoming the inundation and offering to the gods. If you see anything [in the sky], it will be good on this day.

DAY 8: F. F. A. Do not go out at night-time, because Ra goes forth ... As for him who navigates Nun, and as for anybody who is shipwrecked, on water make occasion on water on this day.

DAY 9: F. F. F. If you see anything, it will be good (on this day). It is (the day), of pacifying the heart of those who are in the-horizon in front of the Majesty of Ra.

DAY 10: F. F. F. It is the day of (the going forth of) Hedj-Hotpe (goddess of weaving) while-all gods and goddesses are in festivity. As, to anybody born on this day, he will die as an honoured one in (old age).

DAY 11: A. A. A. Kindle fire on it (i.e. this day). It is the day of-the going forth of the great fire spitting cobra raging in the inaccessible shrine ... Do not look at a bull, and do not make love on this day.

DAY 12: A. A. A. Do not go out on this day. Spend the day until Ra sets in his horizon. It is the day of the crew whom Ra separates from one another. As to anyone disobeying Ra, his house will fall down at once.

DAY 13: F. A. A. Anyone born on this day will die of blindness. It is the day of *Mrt-sm't* (musician goddess perhaps Neith's) massacre.

DAY 14: (NO SPACE) The day of the great Offering (*3'bt*) in the southern heaven (Orion) on this day. Offer to your city gods, for it is pleasant to the gods.

DAY 15: F. A. A. Do not proceed in a boat on this day. It is the day of the rage (in.) the Duat, one shall have no knowledge thereof. Lo, the rowers are on the river on this day. Do not ... (on) this day.

DAY 16: A. A. A. As to anyone born on this day he will die by a crocodile. It is the day of ...... by Neith.

DAY 17: A. A. A. Do not eat any *mehyet*-fish on this day. It is the day of (taking away) Sobek's offering on this day, namely, taking away the offering (from) his mouth on this day.

DAY 18: F. F. F. If you see anything it will be good on this day. It is the day of magnifying the Majesty of Horus more than his brother, which they *(i.e.* the gods) did at the portal.

DAY 19: F. F. F. A happy day in heaven in front of Ra, l. p. h.(life, prosperity and health) the great Ennead is in great festivity. (Burn) incense on the fire for his follower? (in) the Mesektet Mandjet and the gods. It is the day of receiving... It is the day of the going forth... the necropolis before Babai (red eared Baboon) ... his

DAY 20: A. A. A. Do not do any work. It is the day when the great ones followers of Horus and Seth are partial.

DAY 21: F. F. F. Take a holiday on this day; offer to the followers of Ra on this day. Do not kill a bull, and do not let (it) pass before your face (or even) buy it (i.e. the bull) from another one on this day. It is the day to be cautious of it.

DAY 22: A. A. A. Ra calls every god and every goddess, and they await his arrival. He let them enter into his belly. Then they began to move about within him; then he killed them all, then he vomited them into water. They turned into fish, and the souls became birds which flew to heaven. The bodies (became) fish, and the souls (Ba) into birds which are not caught (and) fish on ... as far as this day. Do not eat fish on this day. Do not warm oil; (do not eat) birds.

DAY 23: A. A. A. Do not burn incense on fire for the god on this day. Do not kill any protective (*ʿnḥy*)- serpent (or) any creature among the birds. Do not eat it on this day. Do not listen to singing or dancing on this day. (It is the day of) causing the heart of the enemy of Ra l.p.h. (life, prosperity anf health) to suffer on account of what he has done against his children on this day. As to anyone born on this day he will not live.

DAY 24: F. F. F. The Majesty of this god sails with a favourable wind peacefully ... Behold, he settles down, his heart especially. Then he appeared in the Mesektet-boat, and (then) rising in the Mandjet-boat. As for anyone born on this day (he will die) as an honoured one in old age.

DAY 25: F. F. A. Do not go out of your house on any road at the time of (night). It is the day of the going out of Sekhmet to the eastern district, and of the repelling of the confederates of Seth. As for any lion whom they approach he will pass away at once.

DAY 26: A. A. A. Do not do anything on this day. It is the day of Horus fighting with Seth. Everyone embraced his fellow, and they were on their backs as two men. They were turned into ebony in the Duat... (They spent) three days and four nights in this manner. Then Isis let (a harpoon) down and (it fell) before her son, Horus. He then called with a loud voice saying : 'Behold, (I am her son, Horus).' Then Isis called on this harpoon saying: 'Loosen, loosen from (my) son, Horus.' Thereupon, this harpoon (loosened) from her son, Horus. Then she let down another harpoon which fell in front of Seth. Then he cried saying : 'Behold, I am her brother, Seth.' Then she called on this harpoon: 'Be strong, be strong.' Then this Seth called on her many times saying : 'Do you prefer the foreign man to an uncle?' Then she ... evil ... Then she called on this harpoon saying : 'Loosen, loosen. Behold, my brother of my mother.' Thereupon this harpoon turned away from him. Then they *stood* up as two men, and one turned his back on his fellow. Then the majesty of Horus became angry with his mother, Isis, like a panther. She stood before him...

DAY 27: F. F. F. Peace on the part of Horus with Seth. Do not kill any *protective (ʿnḫy)-* serpent on this day; make a holiday.

DAY 28: F. F. F. The gods are happy on this day when they see (Horus

& Seth) the children of Nut peaceful and content. If you see anything, it will be good on this day.

DAY 29: A. F. F. Do not kindle fire in the house on this day. Do not burn ointment; do not go out by night on this day.

(LAST DAY): F. F. F. If you see anything [in the sky], it will be good on this day.

HOUSE of Ra (tomorrow)

HOUSE of Osiris (yesterday)

HOUSE of Horus (today)

AKHET: INUNDATION SEASON SECOND MONTH

DAY 1: F. F. F. Jubilation - The great Ennead is in festivity on this day. It is the day of establishing the heritage of the Great One.

DAY 2: ?.?.?. The proceeding of the Horus the Elder of Lower Egypt to his mother Neith to see that he was suffering from his buttocks (due to homosexual abuse). Repetition of birth ... great (festivity) in heaven. Offer to all gods. It is important to hear what I say to you.

DAY 3: F. F. F. Thoth in the presence of Ra in the inaccessible shrine. He gave the written order of the reconciliation of the Wedjat-eye; Hu and Sia were among (his) followers ..?.?.. in his manner. If you see anything [in the sky]. It will be good on this day.

DAY 4: A. F. A. Anyone born on this day will die of skin-rash. It is the day of the going forth of Anubis for the inspection of this wabet ($w^{c}bt$) for the protection of the body of the god.

DAY 5: A. A. A. Do not go out of your house on any road on this day. Do not copulate with a woman. It is the day of offering in the presence of the weaver god Hedj-hotpe (and) Montu on this day. Anyone born on this day will die (of) copulation.

DAY 6: F. F. F. A happy day for Ra in heaven, and the gods are pacified in his presence. The Ennead is making glorification in front of the Lord of the Universe. Anyone born on this day will die in a state of drunkenness.

DAY 7: A. A. A. Do not do anything on this day. The going of Ra ... to the countries which he has created in order to kill the children of Bedesh (Apophis) and the return of Ra on (this day)... his neck. Then he killed them before his Ennead. Anyone born on this day will die in foreign lands.

DAY 8: F. F. F. If you see anything on this day it will be good.

DAY 9: F. F. F. Jubilation in the heart of Ra ... His Ennead is in festivity, all enemies are overthrown on this day. Anyone born on this day will die at a good old age.

DAY 10: (F. F. F.). Proceeding of the Majesty of Bastet, mistress of Ankh-towe, and the inquiry of the Majesty of Ra in Heliopolis about her going to pay tribute to the holy tree (upon which royal names are inscribed). It is agreeable to the heart of his followers.

DAY 11: F. F. F. Fixing the front piece at the front of the prow of the barque on this day. Life and prosperity are before the holy tree. Which is established behind him. Everything is good on this day.

DAY 12: A. A. A. It is the day on which he who rebelled against his lord raised his head. His Utterance has annihilated the speech of Seth, son of Nut. The separation of his head is inflicted on him who conspired against his lord.

DAY 13: F. F. F. Satisfying the heart of the great gods with a feast, and saluting their lord who overthrew the enemies, and they will exist no more.

DAY 14: F. F. F. It is the day of receiving the white crown by the Majesty of Horus; his Ennead is in great festivity. Offer to your local gods, and pacify the spirits.

DAY 15: F. A. A. Do not go out of your house at eventide. Going forth of (the Majesty of) Ra at (nightfall with his followers).If any person sees them he will pass away (immediately).

(DAY 16: (......) Feast of (Osiris-Onnophris..), the gods who are in his retinue are in great festivity; the Ennead, their (hearts) being pleased. If you see anything on this day, it will be good.

DAY 17: F. F. F. Smelling ...on this day by the great Ennead and the little Ennead who come forth from Nun. Give up bread and beer. Burn incense to Ra and an invocation-offering to the spirits. It is important so that your words may be listened to by your local gods.

DAY 18: A. A. A. Do not do any (thing) on this day. It is the day Anubis inspected the wabet (w^cbt), while Seth was (making) transformations into lizards in the sight of (all men)... he found. . . being examined to care for burial. Then he started weeping; then he repeated it (i.e. weeping) as he had seen. Thereupon, they started weeping aloud. They placed their hands on their heads; the gods, males and females, likewise.

DAY 19: F. F. F. It is the day of the going forth of Nun to set up the noble one in his place in order to give compensation to the gods who are in the presence of the noble one.

DAY 20: A. A. A. It is the day of giving the compensation in the presence of Ra, and the conducting by Thoth accordingly it is making an example thereof in overthrowing the rebels against their lord. Then they carried off Seth, son of Nut; and they shall be underneath—so said the gods.

DAY 21: A. A. F. It is the day of the going forth of the Upper Egyptian Neith in the presence of the Majesty of (Atum Ra-Hor)akhti—may he live and be prosperous. It is her eyes which guided Thoth in appeasing and praising the Upper Egyptian goddess.

DAY 22: A. A. A. Do not bathe on this day. It is the day of cutting the tongue of the enemy of Sobek, thy son (i.e. son of Neith).

DAY 23: F. A. A. Anyone born on this day will die of a crocodile.

DAY 24: A. A. A. Do not go out of your house on it in any wind until Ra sets. (It is the day) of the going forth of the executioners from Sais of the Delta to look for the children of Bedesh (Apophis) when he is in the ocean. If any lion glances at it (or : them), he will pass away immediately.

DAY 25: A. A. A. (Do not) go out on it (i.e. this day) on any road. It is the day of finding the children of (Apophis) wrapped in [the archaic way] on a mat on (their) sides . . . in his charge... (If any lion) looks for the gods on this day, he will suffer from the trampling of a bull on it (i.e. this day) until he dies.

DAY 26: A. A. A. Do not put the foundation of a house. [See Dreambook III viii 24] Do not put (a ship) in a shipyard. Do not order any work. Do not do any work on this day. It is the day of opening and sealing the windows of the palace of Busiris.

DAY 27: A. A. A. Do not go out. Do not give your back to any work until the sun sets. As to anyone born on this day he will die by a snake,

DAY 28: F. F. F. If you see anything [in the night sky], it will be good on this day.

DAY 29: F. F. F. Anyone born on this day will die as an honourable man among (his people).

LAST DAY: (F. F. F.). . . . . Found missing.(.....) by Nun, father of the gods; the land is in festivity on (this day).

House of Ra (tomorrow)

House of Osiris (yesterday)

House of Horus (today)

AKHET: INUNDATION SEASON THIRD MONTH

DAY 1: F. F. F. Feast of the mistress of heaven, Hathor in heaven ....gods . . . mistress of all female gods.

DAY 2: (BLANK). Return of Wedjoyet from Dep in order to transmit ....

DAY 3: F. F. F. (. . .) by the noble god. If you see anything, it will be good on this day.

DAY 4 : A. A. A. Trembling of the earth under Nun. If anyone navigates on this day, his house (will be destroyed).

DAY 5: A. A. A. Do not keep fire burning in the house on this day. Do not look at it on this day. It is the day of blaming ... by the Majesty of this god.

DAY 6: F. F. F. The encouragement of the gods of the two lands [Horus & Seth] on this day . . .encouragement of ... the whole land (on this day).

DAY 7: F. F. F. If you see anything, (it will be good) on this day.

DAY 8: (NO SPACE) Isis goes forth — her heart being pleased on this day, the heritage being established unto her son, Horus.

DAY 9: A. A. A. Do not go outside on any road from your house on this day. Do not let light fall on your face until Ra sets in his horizon. It is the day of blaming the great ones. FOUND MISSING who were in his presence.

DAY 10: F. F. F. Great rejoicing in heaven; the crew of Ra are in peace, his Ennead is cheerful. Those in the fields are working.

DAY 11: F. F. F. If you see anything, it will be good.

DAY 12: (NO SPACE) The pacification of the heart of the gods wherever they are, the wedjat—eye being on the head of Ra. Fixing ... (for the gods). Raising those who are upon their seats.

DAY 13 : A. A. A. It is the day of cutting into pieces ... ferrymen (?) on the river for not ferrying over the confederates of Seth...any.. .against this neshmet-boat of Osiris which is sailing upstream to Abydos to the great town of Onnophris. Behold, he (sic) is transformed into a little old person in the arms of (his ?) nurse.. .giving gold as a reward to Nemty[16] as a fare saying : Pray, ferry (me) over to the west; then he received it from him...because of announcing the divine limbs. Behold, the confederates were following him like a swarm of reptiles. Thereupon, they (recognised) these gods, while Seth entered into the embalming booth. . .to announce the god's limbs. Then they became fresh. . . he came. . . as enemy on water following him, having transformed themselves into small cattle. Then these gods made a terrible massacre. They divided them among the crew. Then offering was made from the tongue of the enemy of Nemty in order to approach the gold in the house of Nemty to this day. One wondered at the small cattle on the west. One wondered at transforming the small cattle into flocks until this day.

DAY 14: A. A. A. Do not do anything on this day. The heart of the gods is sad because of that which has been done by the enemy of Nemty. Anyone born on this day will die of. . .

DAY 15: A. A. A. Inspecting by Ba-neb-djedet (the lusty bull)... in the sacred temple.

DAY 16 : F. F. F. The appearance of the great ones in Ashmunein. Bringing of Ibis ... establishing ... in Ashmunein. A happy day of infinity and eternity.

DAY 17: A. A. A. (Landing) of the great ones, the upper and lower ones at Abydos; loud weeping and wailing by Isis and Nephthys, her sister, over Onnophris in Sais. It (i.e. weeping and crying) (is heard) in Abydos.

DAY 18: A. A. A. It is the day of the strife by the children of Geb. Seth and sister... Do not approach any road for making a journey on this day.

DAY 19: A. A. A. The children of the storm (Apophis or Seth) of ... Do not sail downstream or upstream on the river. Do not navigate any boat on this day.

DAY 20: A. A. A. The going forth of Bastet, mistress of Ankh-towe in front of Ra, she being angry. The god could not stand in her neighbourhood. Anyone born on this day will die in the year of pestilence.

DAY 21: F. F. F. The feast of Shu, son of Ra. It is the day of Rennutet in the mesektet-boat.

DAY 22: (NO SPACE) Raising Maat in order to see Ra when she is summoned by the gods in the presence of Ra. A uraeus was placed upon her, and another below her, being fixed at the front of the mesektet-boat.

DAY 23: A. A. A. Nun drags .... by their hands out of the fire. Behold, the Majesty of this god judges in that great place ... on the river. Anyone born on this day will not live.

DAY 24: F. F. F. Isis goes forth, her heart being happy and Nephthys being also in jubilation when they see Onnophris ... heart. He has given his throne to his son, Horus in front of Ra.

DAY 25: F. F. F. If you see anything, it will be good on the heart of the gods.

DAY 26: F. F. F. Establishing the Djed of Atum in the heaven and land, of Heliopolis (at the moment) of uproar. Reconciliation of the two lords and causing the land to be in peace. The whole of Egypt is given to Horus, and all the desert land to Seth. Going forth of Thoth in order to judge in the presence of Ra.

DAY 27: F.F.F. Judging Horus and Seth; stopping the fighting. Hunting down the rowers and putting an end to the uproar. Satisfying the two lords and causing the two doors to open.

DAY 28: F. F. F. The gods are in jubilation and in joy when the will is written for Horus, son of Osiris to propitiate Onnophris in the necropolis. Then the land is in festivity and the gods are pleased. If you see anything, it will be good.

DAY 29: F. F. F. The going forth of the three noble ladies who are in the Tanenet sanctuary in the presence of Ptah, beautiful of face, while giving praise to Ra, him who belongs to the throne of truth of the temples of the goddesses. Giving the white crown to Horus, and the red one to Seth.[usually said to be otherway round] Their hearts are pleased there with.

LAST DAY: F. F. F. If you see anything, it will be good on this day.

House of Ra (tomorrow)

House of Osiris (yesterday)

House of Horus (today)

AKHET: INUNDATION SEASON FOURTH MONTH

DAY 1: F. F. F. The great Ennead and the (small) Ennead went to propitiate the Majesty of Nun in the cavern. The Majesty of Thoth ordered Sia and (his followers). . .saying: A copy of the order of the Majesty of Ra saying to his father Nun: This command of the Majesty of Ra Atum is brought to thee. Ra is joyful in his beauty, his Ennead is in festivity. Everybody, every lion and every single one (lit. every nose of his) among the protective (*ʿnḥy*) serpent: gods, goddesses, spirits (akhw), dead and those who came into being in the primordial age, thy form is in every body of thine.

DAY 2: F. F. F. (above line). Gods and goddesses are in festivity; the heaven and the land are in joy. If you see anything [in the sky], (it will be) good on this day.

DAY 3: A. A. A. Do not do anything on this day. It is the day of smashing *(skri)* into the ears of Bata within his own inaccessible temples. Anyone born on this day will die of (his) ears.

DAY 4: F. F. F. One should perform the rituals in the temple of Sokar and in thy house (on) this day, with all provisions in the necropolis — they will be pleasant to the gods on this day.

DAY 5: F. F. F. The going forth of Hathor (Khentet-abet) in the presence of the great ones in the battlefield (Kher-'aha). Life, stability and welfare are given to her and the Ennead and the gods of battlefield; and the Majesty of Inundation, father of the gods, is in great festivity on this day.

DAY 6: A. A. A. (Do not go out on this day). . . when the barque of

Ra (is established) in order to (overthrow Apophis from one moment to another on this) day.

DAY 7: A. A. A. It is the day of... wind...death in... He will turn into...fish. Do not eat or taste (?) mehyet-fish.. on this day.

DAY 8: F. F. F. If you see anything [in the sky], it will be good on this day.

DAY 9: F. F. F. It is the day of the action performed by Thoth. Speech by the Majesty of Ra in the presence of the great ones. Thereupon, these gods together with Thoth caused (Apophis) the enemy of Seth to kill himself in his sanctuary. It is this that has been done by the executioners of Qesert (Apophis) until this day.

DAY 10: F. F. F. As to anyone born on this day (he will die in old age while beer enters into his mouth), his eyes and his face.

DAY 11: F. F. F. Feast of Osiris in Abydos in the great neshmet-boat on this day. The dead are in jubilation.

DAY 12: A. A. A. Do not go out on it (i.e. this day) on any road in the wind. It is the day of the transformation into *Benu*. Offer to the *Benu* in your house on this day

day 13: F. F. F. The going forth of the white one (Hathor) of heaven, their heart being pleased in the presence of Ra. The great Ennead is in festivity. Make a holiday in your house on this day.

DAY 14: F. F. F. The goddesses of weaving (Hedj-hotpe and the Tayet) come forth from the temple of Benben on this day. They handed over things to (Neith) on this day. Their hearts are happy.

DAY 15: ... (Do not)... of... another. *Ndmyt* in order to bring. ...

DAY 16: ...Feast of Sekhmet (and Bastet) in... Ra. Behold.

DAY 17: A. A. F. The people and the gods judge the speech of the crew(?) in Heliopolis when Horus arrives on the battlefield (*Kher-ʿ3hʿ*). Do not go out at midday on this day.

DAY 18 : A. A. A. is the day of overthrowing the boat of the god on this day.

DAY 19 : A. A. A. Presenting of offering in the *Hwt-dsrt*. Making ointment for Osiris before the hall of embalmment. Do not taste bread and beer on this day. Drink water (i.e. juice) of the grapes until Ra sets.

DAY 20 : A. A. A. Do not go out on any road on this day. Do not anoint thyself with ointment on this day. It is the day of looking in the direction of the Akhet-eye (sun). Do not go out of your house at midday.

DAY 21 : A. A. F. It is the day of the going forth of the mysterious great ones to look for the Akhet-eye (sun). Do not go out of your house in day-time.

DAY 22 : F. F. F. If you see anything it will be good on this day. .

DAY 23 : F. F. A. Do not go out during night-time. . . in heaven. . . They. . . in order to annihilate. . . Horus, the saviour of his father. If you see (any lion), you will pass away at his hands (or, immediately).

DAY 25 : missing

DAY 26: . . .F. Thoth establishes the nobles in an advanced position in Letopolis.

DAY 27: F. F. A. If you see anything, it will be good. Do not go out at night-time on this day.

DAY 28: A. A. A. Do not eat any mehyet-fish on this day. Do not offer on it (namely, on this day). It is the day of the going forth of the hat-mehyet-fish which is in Busiris, its form being an iten-fish (i.e. a dolphin).

DAY 29: A. A. A. Do not eat or smell any mehyet-fish while throwing flame into water from what they offer (and which they take upon their hands) of any mehyet-fish (or, any kind of fish).

LAST DAY: F. F. F. If you see anything, it will be pleasing to the heart of the gods and goddesses on this day. Offer to the gods and the assistants of the Ennead. Make an invocation offering to the spirits, and give food in accordance with their list. It is the day of the pleasure of the great Ennead.

House of Ra (tomorrow)

House of Osiris (yesterday)

House of Horus (today)

PERET: WINTER SEASON FIRST MONTH

DAY 1 : F. F. F. Double the offerings and present the gifts of Nehebkau to the gods in the presence of Ptah in the shrines of Ta-nenet of goddesses and gods, saviours of Ra and his own followers, and the. . . of Ptah-Sokar and Sekhmet the great, Nefertem, Horus-Hekenu, Mahes, Bastet, the great fire .... propitiating the Wedjat-eye. It will be good.

DAY 2: F. . . . offering before. . . in. . . nourishment. . . (Make a holiday in your house).

DAY 3: .... Do not burn fire in the presence of Ra , . . . everybody.

DAY 4 : F. F. F. If you see anything, it will be good. Anyone born on this day will die old among his people. He will spend a (long) lifetime, and he would be received by his father.

DAY 5 : F. A. A. It is the day of placing the flame in front of the great ones by Sekhmet who presides in the Lower Egyptian sanctuary when she was violent in her manifestations because of her detention in it (i.e. the sanctuary) by Maat, Ptah, Thoth, Hu and Sia, the gods on this day. . . of everyday on this day.

DAY 6 : F. F. F. Repeat the offerings of the victuals of him who dwells in the holy place (*Weret*), and return the victuals of the noble Khenti-irty, and offerings to the gods were doubled by everyone on this day.

DAY 7: A. A. A. Do not have intercourse with any woman or any person in front of the great flame (i.e. the sun) which is in your house on this day.

DAY 8: F. F. F. If you see anything, it will be good on this day.

DAY 9: F. F. F. The gods are joyful with the offerings of Sekhmet [on this] day. Establish the *cakes of light (pȝwt)*[17] and repeat the offerings. It will be pleasant; to the heart of the gods and the spirits.

DAY 10: A. A. A. (Do not) burn any papyrus on this day. It is the day of the coming forth of flame (together with Horus from the marshes) on this day.

DAY 11: A. A. A. Do not (approach) flame on this day. . . and. . . on this day. . .

DAY 12: A. A. A. If you see any dog (on this day), do not approach him on the day of answering every speech of Sekhmet on this day.

DAY 13: F. F. F. Prolonging life-time and making beneficent the goddess of truth in the temple.

DAY 14: A. A. A. Lamentations of Isis and Nephthys. It is the day when they mourned Osiris in Busiris in remembrance of that which he had seen. Do not listen to singing and chanting on this day.

DAY 15: F. F. F. If you see anything [in the sky], it will be good on this day. It is the day of the going forth of Nun through the cave to the place (where the gods are). . . (in) darkness.

DAY 16 : F. F. F. Going forth of Shu in order to count the crew of the mesektet-boat.

DAY 17: A. A. A. Do not wash yourself with water on this day. It is the day of the going forth of Nun to the place where the gods are. Those who are above and below come into existence; the land being (still) in chaos.

DAY 18: F. F. F. A day (i.e. holiday) in Rostau. The going forth of the gods to Abydos.

DAY 19: A. A. A. The great gods are in heaven on this day and (lit. mixed with) the pestilence of the year. Many deaths are in it (i.e.

this day). If it passes by anyone, he will not recover from the disease which is in him.

DAY 20: A. A. A. Do not do anything on this day. It is the day of the going forth of Bastet who protects the two lands and cares for him who comes in darkness. Beware of passing on land until Ra sets.

DAY 21: F. F. F. Guidance of the two lands by Bastet, and making a Abt-offering to the followers (i.e. of Ra) on this day.

DAY 22: F. F. F. If you see anything [in the sky], it will be good on this day.

DAY 23: F. F. F. Anyone born on this day will die in great old age and rich in every good thing.

DAY 24: F. F. F. Everything has been placed behind him in the presence of the (Ennead) (on) the occasion of being loyal to the executioners of Ra. Happiness is in heaven and on earth on this day.

DAY 25: (NO SPACE) Do not eat milk on this day. Establishing of the great divine cow in the presence of the Majesty of Ra. Drink and eat honey on this day.

DAY 26: A. A. A. Do not go out on it (*i.e.* this day) until Ra sets when offerings are diminished in Busiris, while they are put on earth towards heaven. They will be much blamed about it.

DAY 27: F. F. F. Great festivity in Hefau. . .??. . .in festivity. . . on this day.

DAY 28: F. F. F. (of Horus & Seth not to fight) taking a solemn oath by Thoth in Ashmunein, and the going forth of the noble one. The land is in festivity on this day. Make a holiday in your house.

DAY 29: F. F. F. Appearance in the sight of Hu. Thoth will send this command southwards to guide the two lands by Bastet together with the sole mistress, Sekhmet the great, the gods being happy. If you see anything, it will be good on this day.

LAST DAY: F. F. F. Crossing over in the presence of Nun from the temple of Hapi, the father of the gods and the Ennead, Lords of the Battlefield (Kher-'aha). Do not neglect them while incense is on the fire according to their list *on* this day.

House of Ra (tomorrow)

House of Osiris (yesterday)

House of Horus (today)

PERET: WINTER SEASON SECOND MONTH

DAY 1: F. F. F. The gods and goddesses are in festivity on this day, (namely), in the feast of (lifting) the heaven of Ra by Ptah with his hands (he who has no equal). A holiday in the entire land.

DAY 2: F.F.F. The day of receiving Ra by the gods. The heart of the two lands is in festivity.

DAY 3: A. A. A. Do not go out of your house on any road on this day. (It is the day of) the going forth of Seth together with his confederates to the eastern horizon, and the navigation of Maat to the place (where the gods are).

DAY 4: F. F. F. Apply your heart to your local gods; propitiate your spirits (akhw); exalt your crew during the day on this day.

DAY 5: F. F. F. If you see anything [in the sky], it will be good on this day.

DAY 6: A. A. A. It is the day of putting up the Djed by the Majesty of Osiris. Then the gods were sad with (their) faces downwards when they remember the Majesty of this god. They pronounced those who were before.

DAY 7: F. F. F. Make invocation offering to the spirits (akhw) in your house. Make the great (3^cbt) offering to the gods, and they will be accepted on this day.

DAY 8: F. F. F. Make a holiday in Letopolis. The gods and goddesses are in festivity on this day.

DAY 9: F. F. F. The god enters as he will conduct this rationing and all the gods of the battlefield *(Kher-ʿ3h3)*. If you see anything [in the sky], it will be good on this day.

DAY 10: A. A. A. The going forth of the Wedjat-eye for singing in Heliopolis. Raising up of the (female) Majesty of the sanctuary by Mnevis. Ra raised Maat again and again to Atum.

DAY 11: F. F. F. Feast of Neith in Sais, and taking the writing material that was prepared in her house. The going forth of Sobek to guide her Majesty. Thou wilt see good (at) her hands.

DAY 12: F. F. F. If you see anything, it will be good on this day.

DAY 13: A. A. A. Do not go out of your house on any road on this day. It is the day of the proceeding of Sekhmet to Letopolis (?) Her great executioners passed by the offering of Letopolis on this day.[15]

DAY 14: A. F. F. Do not go out on it (i.e. this day) at the beginning of dawn. It is the day of seeing the rebel (Apophis) and killing him by Seth at the prow of the great barque.

DAY 15: (APPARENTLY BLANK) The gods go forth for him in heaven. His two hands holding the *ankh* and *was* which he gives to *Khenty-irty* at the time of his reckoning.

DAY 16: (B L A N K) ...Awakening of Isis by the Majesty of Ra... their hands when the son Horus saved his father. He has beaten Seth and his confederates.

DAY 17: F. F. F. It is the day of keeping those things of the *wabet* of Osiris which have been placed in the hands of Anubis.

DAY 18: A. A. A. The going forth of the seven executioners in R-hesert, their fingers are searching for the Akhet-eye in the town of Iyet and Letopolis.

DAY 19: F. A. A. Do not decide yourself to go during daytime. It is the day of (mourning the god), (blank)

SUPERNATURAL ASSAULT IN ANCIENT EGYPT

DAY 20: A. A. A. The proceeding of the (female) Majesty of heaven southward to the road...

DAY 21 : (BLANK) Birth of the cattle. . . to the place where the meadows are in the neighbourhood of this foremost god.

DAY 22: F. F. F. If you see anything [in the sky], it will be good on this day.

DAY 23: F. F. F. If you see anything [in the sky], it will be good on this day.

DAY 24: A. A. A. Do not sail in a boat on this day. The gods are descending into the river. As to anyone who approaches on it (i.e. this day) on the river, he will not live.

DAY 25: F. F. F. If you see anything [in the sky], it will be good (on this day).

DAY 26 : (BLANK) Going forth of Min from Coptos on this day. He is guided to it; boasting about his beauty (phallus?). Isis saw that his face was beautiful.

DAY 27: (NO SPACE) Feast of Sokar in Rostau before (that of) Onnophris in Abydos.

DAY 28: F. F. F. Onnophris is pleased and the spirits are joyful, the dead are also in festivity.

DAY 29: A. A. A. Instigation of fighting, creation of rebellion and making uproar among the children of Geb. Do not do anything on this day.

LAST DAY: A. A. A. Do not raise your voice on this day.

House of Ra (tomorrow)

House of Osiris (yesterday)

House of Horus (today)

PERET: WINTER SEASON THIRD MONTH

DAY 1: F. F. F. It is the day of ... in heaven and on earth and everybody likewise. Feast of entering into heaven and the two banks. Horus is jubilating.

DAY 2: F. F. F. If you see anything [in the sky], it will be (good on) this day.

DAY 3: . . . (blank) . . .

DAY 4: F. A. A. Announcement of fighting; call in Heliopolis by Seth; his voice being in heaven, his voice being on earth, through great fury.

DAY 5: F. F. F. Neith goes forth from Sais when they see (her) beauty in the night for four and half (hours). Do not go out in them (i.e. these hours).

DAY 6: F. F. F. Jubilation of Osiris in Busiris; going forth of Anubis, (his) adorers (or, adoration) following him; he has received everybody in the hall. Mayest thou make the ritual

DAY 7: A. A. A. Do not go out of your house until Ra sets. It is the day when *the* eye of Ra called the followers, and they reached him (in) the evening. Beware of it!

DAY 8: F. F. F. If you see anything [in the sky], it will be good on this day. It is the day *of* making way for the gods by Khnum who presides over those who remove themselves from him.

DAY 9: F. F. F. Judgement in Heliopolis.

DAY 10: A. A. A. It is the day of the coming of Thoth. They guided the very great Flame (Nesert) into her house of the desert of eternity (along) the way which she has found among them. As to anyone who approaches her on this day, thou (sic) shalt not be separated from her by violence.

DAY 11: F. F. F. As to the dead who go about in the necropolis on this day, the dead are (going about) in order to repel the anger of the enemy who is in the said land.

DAY 12: F. F. F. The Nile *(wsr-hat)* comes from Nun on this day. Victuals are being given on this day.

DAY 13: F. F. F. Coming of Thoth (with his spirits) on this day. Replacing ... in the seats of the goddesses. As to any ritual action, it will be good on this day.

DAY 14: A. A. (SIC) Do not go out of your house (on any road) on this day. It is the day of making health (the life time in Letopolis).

DAY 15: A. A. A. Rebellion in the shrine (?) Do not do any work on this day.

DAY 16: A. A. A. Opening of the windows and opening of the court, and looking into the doorways of Karnak, where his place is. Do not see darkness on this day.

DAY 17: A. A. A. Do not pronounce the name of Seth on this day. As to him who pronounces his name without his knowledge, he will not stop from fighting in his house eternally.

DAY 18: F. F. F. Feast of Nut who counts the days. Make a holiday (in) your house.

DAY 19: (NO SPACE) Birth of Nut anew ... (good) any dead on (this) day. . . Bastet. . . the Majesty of the foreign land. Do not go out of your house; do not see light.

DAY 20: A. A. A. Do not go out of your house on any road. Do not see light *(sw)*.

(DAY 21: dropped).

DAY 22: A. A. A. Birth of the mysterious one (Apophis) with his limbs. Do not get the thought of pronouncing the name of the snakes. It is the day of catching his children in Dep.

DAY 23: F. F. F. Feast of Horus in *kem-wer* on this day of his years in his very beautiful images.

DAY 24: A. A. A. Do not go out of your house on any road on this day.

DAY 25: (NO SPACE) Do not do anything on this day because -of the great cry which the gods of Djesert-(places) made, having come this day.

DAY 26: A. A. A. He was sent into the cave without the knowledge of the great ones (?)... to look for the occasion of coming on this day.

DAY 27: A. A. A. Do not do anything on this day.

DAY 28: F. F. F. (Feast of) Osiris in Abydos. The Majesty of Onnophris puts up the *twryt-tree*.

DAY 29: F. F. F. If you see anything, it will be good.

LAST DAY:... Feast in Busiris. The names of the doorways (of the horizon) come into existence.

House of Ra (tomorrow)

House of Osiris (yesterday)

House of Horus (today)

PERET: WINTER SEASON FOURTH MONTH

DAY 1: F. F. F. Great feast (in heaven). It is the day of smiting the enemy as rebels against their mistress on this day.

DAY 2: F. F. F. The Majesty of Geb proceeds to the throne of Busiris to see Anubis, who commands the council on the requirements (of the day).

DAY 3: A. A. A. Do not do anything on this day. Fighting of the great ones with the Uraeus, appointing her on the spot to make grow (lit. create) this eye of Horus the Elder. As for any lion who pronounces the name of the Decan-Orion he will pass away at once.

DAY 4: F. F. F. If you see anything, it will be good on this day. The gods and goddesses are satisfied when they see the children of Geb sitting in their places.

DAY 5: A. A. A. The Majesty of Horus is well when the Red Goddess sees his form. As for anybody who approaches on it (i.e. this day), anger will start on it (i.e. this day).

DAY 6: A. A. A. Going forth of the stars, (culminating) bitterly and openly. If anybody sees the small cattle, he will pass away at once.

DAY 7: F. F. F. (The going forth) of Min into the tent, 1. p. h. (life, prosperity and health) in festivity. The gods are jubilating. Pay attention to the incense on the fire. Smell (or, smelling of) sweet myrrh.

DAY 8: F. F. F. The Ennead is in adoration when (they see) this eye of (Horus) the Elder in its place. Revised are all its parts (½, ¼ etc) in it in counting it for its master.

DAY 9: A. A. A. Do not go out on it (at the time of) darkness when (Ra) goes in it... its name... (lacuna). It is the day of... (introducing) the great ones before Ra (to the wholeness of the *wedjet*) ... (If) you see (anything, it will be good on this day). (Do not) go out of your house (on any road) on this day.

DAY 11: A. A. A. .. (gods) of the shrines in the temple ....

DAY 12: A. A. A. As to him who sees dancing, or digging on any road... do not approach (?) the Majesty of Montu... in digging (or dancing) and do not look at it at all ...

DAY 13: A. A. A. ... .any wind on this day. It is the day of conducting Osiris. . . his ship to Abydos (on this day).

DAY 14: A. A. A. The crew go about the gods on this day to look for (the confederates of Seth). Do not be courageous (on this day).

DAY 15: F. F. F. A great happy day in the eastern horizon of heaven when instructions were given to the followers of the gods in their temples in the presence of the great ones in the two horizons.

DAY 16: F. F. F. Going forth of Khepra who hears the words of his followers there. Every town is in joy.

DAY 17: A. A. A. Going forth of Seth, son of Nut, to disturb the great ones who check him in his town of *Sw* (in Heracleopolitan nome). Now these gods recognized him, and they repelled his followers, none of them remained.

DAY 18: A. A. A. Do not approach (when the Majesty of) Ra goes forth. Do not wash yourself with water on this day.

DAY 19: F. F. F. The Majesty of (Ra) goes forth (in his barque. . .) heaven. Feast. . . in Heliopolis. (If you see anything, it will be) good on this day.

DAY 20: A. A. A. Do not (do any work on) this day while he (repels those who rebel) against their master. As to anyone who passes (them, he will suffer from the trampling of a bull *herey-ka*) to infinity.

DAY 21: A. A. A. Do not go out on it on (any road on this day).

DAY 22: A. A. A. Anyone born on this day will not live. It is the day (of killing) the children of Bedesh (Apophis).

DAY 23: A. A. F. It is the day of offering . . . Abydos, (victuals) . . . invocation offering to the spirits (akhw).

DAY 24: A. A. A. (Do not mention the name of) Seth in (a loud voice) on this day. It is the day of (the rebellion) which he has done (against) Onnophris. As to anyone who mentions his name forgetfully, fighting (is made) in his house (for ever).

DAY 25: A. A. A. (Do not eat anything) which is on water. It is the day of cutting from the tongue of Sobek (in his Sethian aspect) on this day.

DAY 27: A. A. A. Do not go out of your house until Ra sets because the Majesty of the goddess Sekhmet is angry in the land of Temhu. Behold she went about, walking and standing (or, waiting) ...

DAY 28: F. F. F. If you see anything [in the sky], it will be good on this day.

DAY 29: F. F. F. The gods are satisfied (when) they give adoration to Onnophris, incense being on the fire, and your local gods. . . myrrh. . . pleasant on (this day).

LAST DAY: F. F. F. Offer to. . . Ptah-Sokar-Osiris. . . Atum, lord of the two lands (of Heliopolis). . . to all the gods. . . on this day.

House of Ra (tomorrow)

House of Osiris (yesterday)

House of Horus (today)

SHEMU: HARVEST SEASON FIRST MONTH

DAY 1: F. F. F. (Feast of Horus), (son of) Isis and his followers ... day ...

DAY 2: A. A. A. Do not (sail ?) in any wind on this day.

DAY 3: F. F. F. If (you see any) thing, (it will be good on this day).

DAY 4: A. A. A. (Do not go out) of your house (on any) road on this day. It is the day of... year. Follow Horus on this day.

DAY 5: A. A. A. Feast of Ba-neb-djedet (on this day) ...(As to any who goes out of his house on this day, disease abandons him until) he dies.

DAY 6: F. F. F. Coming of the great ones from the House of Ra rejoicing on this day when they receive the Wedjat-eye together with their followers. If you see anything, it will be good on this day.

DAY 7: F. F. F. The crew follow Horus in the foreign land, examining its list therein when he smote him who rebelled against his master. Every land is happy, and their heart is glad ...

DAY 8: (NO SPACE). If you see anything, it will be good on this day.

DAY 9: F. F. F. If you see anything [in the sky], it will be good on this day ... Ennead.

DAY 10: A. A. A. Proceeding of the white one (Hathor) of heaven upstream to seek at the front among (those who rebelled against their) master in the Delta.

DAY 11: found missing... (in his attendance)... Holy House (*ḥwt-dsrt*).

DAY 12: A. A..A Do not... he goes forth .. his body...

DAY 13: ... F. ... Do not... to (or, until).

DAY 14: A. A. A. ... Apophis in... cutting into (or, from) (the tongue of the enemy of) Sobek (on this day). It is the day of... his head by...

DAY 15: A. A. A. (Any one born on this day) he will die... Do not go out of your house until Ra sets) in the horizon...

DAY 16: F. ...F (you see anything on this day)... (If you see anything, it will be good (on this day)... The Ennead is in joy and the crew (of Ra) is in festivity.

DAY 17: missing

DAY 18:

DAY 19: F. F. F. It is the day of counting in the presence of (?) by Thoth who heard Maat, this great one. All gods are in great festivity.

DAY 20: A. A. A. Maat judges in front of these gods who became angry in the island of the sanctuary of Letopolis. The Majesty of Horus revised it.

DAY 21: A. A. A. Vomiting the things which come back from the boat, so that no follower of Ra remains, namely, his followers (who are) in his attendance.

DAY 22: F. F. F. Anyone born on this day will die in old age...

DAY 23: F. F. F. If you see anything, (it will be good on this day).

DAY 24: words of (?) the rebels ...on this day ......

DAY 26: F. F. F. If you see anything, it will be good on this day).

DAY 27: A. A. A. .. Babai... (in) front of Ra...

DAY 28: F. F. F. . . . great. . . him on this day. . .If you see anything, (it will be good on this day). . .

(LAST DAY) : F. F. F. Feast of. . . happy.

House of Ra (tomorrow)

House of Osiris (yesterday)

House of Horus (today)

SHEMU: HARVEST SEASON SECOND MONTH

DAY 1: F. F. F. ...... Osiris ...... gods(?)

DAY 2: [MISSING] Oh heart of the gods, listen very well—FOUND MISSING. The crew of Ra is in festivity.

DAY 3: F. F. F. The month of the followers of Ra. A day is fixed in heaven and on earth as a feast.

DAY 4: A. A. A. Do not shout at anybody on this day while that which Geb and Nut have done is counted in the presence (lit. on the hands) of the gods.

DAY 5: F. F. F. If you see anything, it will be good on this day.

DAY 6: (NO SPACE) Horus proceeds to repel what was done against his father and to inquire from the followers of his father Onnophris on this day.

DAY 7: A. A. A. Do not go out of your house during waking-time. . . Ra in the horizon. It is the day of the executioners of Sekhmet. (counting) by names.

DAY 8: F. F. F. Make a holiday for Ra and his followers make a good day on this day.

DAY 9: F. F. F. Make incense of (different kinds of) sweet herbs for his followers (while pleasing) him on this day.

DAY 10: F. F. F. Anyone (born) on this day (he) will be noble.

DAY 11: A. A. A. Do not sail in a boat on the river. It is the day of catching birds and fish (by) the followers of Ra. (Anyone who sails) on the river he will not live.

DAY 12: F. F. F. If you see anything, it will be good on this day.

DAY 13: F. F. F. Feast of Wedjat in (settlement of) Dep, and her followers are (also) in festival when singing and chanting take place on the day of offering the incense (and all kinds of sweet herbs).

DAY 14: F. F. F. If you see anything, it will be good on this day.

DAY 15: A. A. A. Do not judge yourself... On this day. It is the day of fighting... their rebellion.

DAY 16: F. F. F. Anyone born on this day he will die great as a magistrate among all people.

DAY 17: A. A. A. Do not go out on it. Do not do anything, or any work on this day.

DAY 18: A. A. A. Do not eat the meat of any lion. It is the day of the going forth of Khenti (Osiris) of the god's house when he goes about to the holy mountain. All those who will smell death and skin rash will not recover.

DAY 19: A. A. A. The Ennead sails, they are much (i.e. numerous sailings of the Ennead) in the entire land. If any lion is seen, he will pass away at once. It is the day of judging the great ones on this day.

DAY 20: A. A. A. Many die when they come with adverse wind. Do not go out with any wind on this day.

DAY 21: A. A. F. It is the day of the (decan) the Leg (w'rty) the children of Nut (epagomenal days). Do not go out on it until daybreak (i.e. the ninth hour).

DAY 22: A. A. A. Disturbance below and uproar of the gods of the *kri-* shrines on this day when Shu was complaining (?) to Ra about the great ones of infinity. Do not go out on it.

DAY 23: F. F. F. The crew rest when they see the enemy of their master.

DAY 24: F. F. F. If you see anything [in the sky], (it will be) good on this day.

DAY 25: F. F. F. Pacified are the Akhet-eye, everything and everybody. It is pleasant to the gods and Ra.

DAY 26: A. A. A. The going forth of Neith. She treads on this day in the flood (in order to) look for things of Sobek. If any lion sees them, he will pass away immediately.

DAY 27: A. A. A. The cutting of the heads and the tying of the throats and the occurrence of the flight among the gods on this day. Do not (do) any work on this day.

DAY 28: F. F. F. Purifying things and offerings in Busiris. The gods spend the day in festivity. Act in accordance with that which happens (i.e. the event) on this day.

DAY 29: F. F. F. If you see anything, it will be good on this day.

LAST DAY: F. F. F. The going forth of Shu with the intention to bring back the Wedjat-eye, and appeasing Thoth on this day.

House of Ra (tomorrow)

House of Osiris (yesterday)

House of Horus (today)

SHEMU: HARVEST SEASON THIRD MONTH

DAY 1: F. F. F. A great feast in the southern heaven, every land and everybody start jubilating. The mistress of heaven, *Ipt-hmt* (Hippo) *and* every land are in festivity on this day.

DAY 2: F. F. F. Every god and every goddess spend the day in festivity and in great astonishment in the sacred temple.

DAY 3: A. A. A. Anger of the divine-Majesty. Do not do anything on this day.

DAY 4: F. F. F. If you see anything, it will be good on this day.

DAY 5: A. A. A. Do not go out of your house. Do not proceed on a boat. Do not do any work on it. It is the day of the departure of this goddess to the place wherefrom she came. The heart of the gods is sad about them very much.

DAY 6: A. A. A. Do not fight or make uproar. . . in your house while every temple of the goddess is in (or like) this manner.

DAY 7: A. A. A. Sailing of the gods after the Majesty of the goddess. As for. . . on (or, in) it. . . A flame which takes place in front of everybody on this day.

DAY 8: A. A. A. Do not beat anybody. Do not strike anybody. It is the day of the massacre of the followers of the Majesty of the goddess.

DAY 9: F. F. F. The gods are content and they are happy because Ra is at peace with the Akhet-eye. Every god is in festivity on this day.

DAY 10: A. A. A. Creating enmity according to the event. The gods who are in the shrine, their hearts are sad.

DAY 11: A. A. A. Introducing the great ones by Ra to the booth to see what he had observed through the eye of Horus the Elder. They were with heads bent down when they saw an eye of Horus being angry in front of Ra. Do not perform any ritual on this day.

DAY 12: F. F. F. Holiday... Reception of Ra, (his) followers are in festivity, and everybody is in festivity.

DAY 13 : A. A. A. The Majesty of this god proceeds sailing westwards to see the beauty of Onnophris on this day.

DAY 14 : A. A. A. Do not burn on this day in your house with anything (in the way) of burning flame with any of its glow on that day of the anger of that eye of Horus the Elder.

DAY 15: F. F. F. If you see anything, it will be good. Horus hears your words in the presence of every god and every goddess on this day. You will see every good thing in your house.

DAY 16: A. A. A. It is the day of transmitting Maat to the shrine by the Majesty of Ra in the Heliopolis of Ra. These gods learnt that she was much blamed for it.

DAY 17: A. A. A. The escape of the fugitive (eye)... and the gods became deprived of Ra who had come to hand over the rebels to him ... in their path.

DAY 18: A. A. A. Do not go out of your house on any road on this day. The going forth of Maat and Ra... secret on this day. If anyone... outside... this trampling of a bull ...

DAY 19: A. A. A. Do not 'shake hands' on this day nor do any work on this day. Breaking of... into (or, through) water on this day.

DAY 20: A. A. A. Do not go out of your house on any road on this day.

DAY 21: F. F. F. If you see anything [in the sky], it will be good on this day.

DAY 22: A. A. A. Do not see any digging, any skin-rash or any fever on this day. It is the day of Sepa in Tura coming from Heliopolis.

DAY 23: A. A. A. Anyone born on this day will not live. It is the day of quarrelling and reproaching with Onnophris on this day.

DAY 24: F. F. F. It is the day of... children of Bedesh (Apophis). The gods killed them when he came. Then he sailed to the south.

DAY 25: F. A. F. Do not go out at midday; the great enemy (Apophis) is in the temple of Sekhmet.

DAY 26: F. F. F. If you see anything, it will be good on this day.

DAY 27: A. A. A. Do not go out of your house on this day. It is the day of sailing on the river, and of overthrowing the enclosure wall.

DAY 28: A. A. A. Creating misery, and bringing terror into existence in conformity with the custom of what is in the year.

DAY 29: F. F. F. The feast of Mut in Shera (the sacred lake at Karnak) on this day. It is the day of feeding the gods and her followers on this day.

LAST DAY: F. F. F. If you see anything [in the sky], it will be good on this day.

House of Ra (tomorrow)

House of Osiris (yesterday)

House of Horus (today)

SHEMU: HARVEST SEASON FOURTH MONTH

DAY 1: F. F. F. Transmitting the Great (*ꜣḫt*) offerings (to) those who are in heaven. Every god and every goddess spend the day in the feast of Onnophris on this day.

DAY 2: F. F. F. Truth... (and all gods) perform the rites as one who is in heaven (i.e. Onnophris) day

DAY 3: A. A. A. (Proceeding of the Majesty of this goddess) to Heliopolis of Ra. A (feast) was made (on this day). Do not go out in order to do anything on this day.

DAY 4: A. A. F. It is the day of the procession of Sopdu (Sirius) together with his followers, being in a state of youth and remaining in the course of the day. Never will she be able to find a living soul.

DAY 5: F. F. F. 'Letopolis' (Maner) is in festivity, Min being at Akhmim. If you see anything, it will be good on this day.

DAY 6: A. A. A. Transmitting the rejuvenated one in Restau and hiding (the mysteries) of the conspirators on this day. (Do not do) anything on this day.

DAY 7: A. A. A. The dead one goes about in the necropolis and comes on earth. As to him who approaches him, he will suffer from the trampling of a bull and will not recover until he dies.

DAY 8: F. F. F. If you see anything, it will be good on this day.

DAY 9: F. F. F. Anyone born on this day will have noble honour.

DAY 10: F. F. F. It is the repulsion of the crew who was (in) the

Delta. It is the day of the entering of the eye of Ra into his horizon when he sees his beauty.

DAY 11: A. A. A. Causing disturbance in the presence of the followers of Ra, and repelling the confederates of Seth into the eastern country.

DAY 12: F. F. F. Jubilation throughout the entire land on this day. The heart of those who are in the shrine is happy.

DAY 13: F. F. F. A holiday because of defending the son of Osiris. . . back of the portal by Seth.

DAY 14: F. F. F. Establishing her seat and hall. . . god portal (on the) first (occasion) on this day.

DAY 15: A. A. A. Do not do (any) thing. Do not go out on any road on this day. . . going forth of Ra to, propitiate Nun. . . in his cavern (in front of) his followers and the Ennead of the mesektet-barque on this day

DAY 16: F. F. F. . . . to give water to those who are (in) the underworld Ennead of the west. It is pleasant to your father and your mother who are in the necropolis.

DAY 17: F. F. F. If you see anything, it will be good on this day.

DAY 18: A. A. F. Do not go out at the time of the morning because of the crew who leads (or, is leading) the rebels. If any lion goes out on earth on this day (he) will be blind, and they will say: he will not live.

DAY 19: F. F. F. Celebrate your feast of your god. Appease your spirit (akh), for this Eye of Horus has returned complete, nothing is missing in it.

DAY 20: A. A. A. Do not kill a guardian serpent on this day. It is the day of the cleaning and revision of the noble ones. There is silence because of it on earth in order to propitiate the Wedjat-eye on this day.

DAY 21: F. F. F. If you see anything, it will be good on this day.

DAY 22: F. F. F. The feast of Anubis who is on his mountain on this day. The children of [Geb] and Nut spend the day in festivity, which is a holiday after the good bath of the gods on this day.

DAY 23: A. A. A. Do not taste bread or beer on this day because the... of that which was done before him who rebelled against his master on this day.

DAY 24: F. F. F. Make Great (3^cbt) offerings to the gods in the presence of Ra. Make a holiday in your house.

DAY 25: F. F. F. The god is ... established in front of the crew of Ra who is happy in the Holy House ($hwt\text{-}dsrt$).

DAY 26: F. A. F. Do not go out on it at midday. The gods . . . (sail) with all winds. . . takes place. . . (Do not) go out of your house

DAY 27: A. A. A. . . . earth. Do not do anything on it.

DAY 28: F. F. F. . . . (Feast) on Min. Day of. . . If (you see anything), it will be good on this day.

DAY 29: F. F. F. .. Holiday in the temple of Sokar, in the estate of Ptah, and those who are in this estate are in great festivity, being healthy.

LAST DAY: F. F. F. .. Anything which comes forth on it in the estate of Ptah will be good. As for anything (or, offering), any rite or anybody on this day, it is good throughout the year. Sing and offer much.

THE FIVE DAYS ADDITIONAL TO THE YEAR

The great ones are born. As for the great ones whose forms are not mysterious, beware of them. Their occasion (or, deed) will not come... They have proceeded.

BIRTH OF OSIRIS,

BIRTH OF HAROERIS,

BIRTH OF SETH,

BIRTH OF ISIS,

BIRTH OF NEPHTHYS.

AS TO ANYONE WHO KNOWS THE NAME OF THE FIVE EPAGOMENAL DAYS, he does not hunger, he does not thirst, Bastet does not overpower him. He will not enter into the great law court, he will not die through an enemy of the king and will not die (or, depart) through the pestilence of the year. But he will last every day (till) death arrives, whereas no illness will take possession of him.

AS TO HIM WHO KNOWS THEM, *Hw* will be prosperous within him, his speech is important to listen to in the presence of Ra.

FIRST DAY : THE BIRTH OF OSIRIS.

WORDS TO BE SAID ON IT:

O Osiris, bull in his cavern (whose) name is hidden ... offspring (?) of his mother. Hail to thee, hail to thee (??). I am (thy son)... O father, Osiris.

THE NAME OF THIS DAY: The pure one, field

SECOND DAY : THE BIRTH OF HORUS. WORDS TO BE SAID ON IT :

O Horus, (*khenty-irty*) of Letopolis. It is repeated anew mighty of strength, master of fear, save me from bad and evil things and from any slaughter. Horus, son of Geb

THE NAME OF THIS DAY: powerful is the heart

THIRD DAY : THE BIRTH OF SETH. WORDS TO BE SAID ON IT:

OH, SETH, Son of Nut, great of strength, save me from bad and evil things and from any slaughter, protection is at thy hands of thy holiness. I am the son of thy son.

THE NAME OF THE DAY : It is powerful of heart.

FOURTH DAY : THE BIRTH OF ISIS. WORDS TO BE SAID ON IT:

Oh, this Isis, daughter of Nut the eldest, mistress of magic, provider (?) of the book, mistress who appeases the two lands, her face is glorious. I am the brother and the sister.

THE NAME OF THE DAY : He who makes terror.

FIFTH DAY : THE BIRTH OF NEPHTHYS. WORDS TO BE SAID ON IT :

Oh, Nephthys, daughter of Nut, sister of Seth, she whose father sees a healthy daughter, beautiful of face. Beautiful of face. I am the divine power in the womb of my mother Nut.

THE NAME OF THE DAY: The child who is in his nest.

WORDS TO BE SAID AFTER THEM WHEN THE EPAGOMENAL DAYS ARE COMPLETED.

Hail to you! O great ones according to their names, children of a goddess who have come forth from the sacred womb, lords because of their father, goddesses because of their mother, without knowing the necropolis. Behold, may you protect (me) and save me. May you make me prosperous, may you make protection, may you repeat and may you protect me. I am one who is on their list.

THIS SPELL IS TO BE SAID FOUR TIMES.

Make for thyself an amulet as protection, [drawn on fine linen] and placed about the neck (for the five) epagomenal days in (the name of) these gods on the day. . . written on the choice of. . . amulet. . . THE FEMALE FIGURE of Isis, THE FEMALE FIGURE of Nephthys . . .

BLACK COLOUR ANOINTED WITH FIRST CLASS OIL AND FUMIGATED WITH INCENSE ON A BURNER. THEY SHOULD BE PURIFIED, LOOSENED, AND THROWN INTO WATER for the father Nun and for the mother Nut after the day of the birth of Ra and act. Behold, make for thyself a big *ꜣꜥbt* of bread, beer, oxen, fowl, carob beans incense *ty-sps-wood* and all kinds of dates and vegetables — being clean, being clean in front of Ra-Harakhti when he shines in the eastern horizon of heaven and when he sets in the western horizon. Behold, thou bathest in the fresh water ... of the beginning of inundation. Paint thine eyes with green paint; take a drink of wine and anoint thyself...

Notes

1. Kákosy, L (1982) 'Decans in Late Egyptian Religion' *Oikumene* 3 pp163-191. (p.188)

2. Kákosy, L, *op cit*

3. S18 in Gardiner's sign list

4. Assmann 2001 : 194

5. Edwards IES (1960) *Hieratic Papyri In the British Museum*, 4th series - Amuletic Decrees, BM

   Example L2 gives further examples of potential threats to the newborn these include, Khonsu, Sekhmet, Hathor (the Negress of Nekheb in T3), Amun, Mut, Montu etc; the seven stars of the Great Bear (HpS) ie Seth; safe from meteorites (see the Tale of Shipwrecked Sailor); P3 v 8-9 against physicians; L3 Bastet, the Decanals and seasonal gods; disease entities; T2 rt 10-13 - against evil sleep; Examples T1 15.20 in Edwards (1960) make every dream good, and the dreams people have of you likewise good. C1 57-61 a personal book of fate is often mentioned - probably kept by Khonsu because of his association with time.

6. Owner: Buiruharkhons, d. of Djedkhons (m.) and p. V Provenance: Not recorded; probably Thebes.

   Length: 0-65 m. Width: 0-06 m.

   Date of acquisition: 1856 (from L. Vassalli Bey).

7. The special baboon avatars of Khonsu are mentioned several times (Khonsu-unnekhen & Khonsu-pairsekheru). They appear as outriders for the main god Amun in his Karnak shrine and are perhaps related to dark and light moon. Perhaps because this is Thebes and Khonsu is the child of Amun & Mut - these baboons have some special relationship to childhood.

8. Khonsu issues the decree and is also included among the dangers.

9. Origen, Celsum viii 58 asserts that the Egyptians regard the Decan gods as protector of the 36 parts of the body; viz: head, hands and fingers, sides, abdomen, gentrials, rectum, perineum, thighs, shins, toes, soles of feet.

10. Spalinger 1991; First publication of Cairo Papyrus by Bakir (1960); the standard source now Troy 1987; Vernus, P (1981) 'Omina Calendériques et Comptabilité d'offrandes sur une tablette Hiératique de la XVIIIe Dynastie' RDE 33 pp.89-124.for comparable wooden tablet with patronesses of each month; Bács, Tamás A (1987) 'Prolegomena to the study of Calendars of Lucky and Unlucky Days' in Roccati, A (1987).

11. Schott, Siegfried (1950) *Altägyptische Festdaten*

12. Troy 1987: 139

13. Troy *op cit*

14. This tripartite version uses a permutation very reminiscent of 'knuckle bone oracles'.

15. See II Peret 19 for an example of the seven executioners.

16. Written with rare horizontal use of the determinative D51 'finger' so presumably Antj but elsewhere is nmtj - nemty - a form of Seth. See Lexikon under 'Ante'

17. pawet (pAwt) is some sort of offering cake - and refers to a primeval god - ie perhaps one of the archaic beings of Egypt's 'first creation'. So literally some sort of 'god cake' comparable to the occult eucharist or 'cakes of light'. This is a very early reference to the offering cakes described in for instance Plutarch 362, 30 - which were stamped with an image of Seth before consumption or use as an offering. See Darby, W J (1977) Food: the gift of Osiris, Academic press., for what little info there is on ancient Egyptian offering cakes.

5. Supernatural Assault

> 'Infatuated by our own clever minds, we turned our backs on the old redeeming symbols. We forgot that the symbolic is that which holds together – it is the very meaning of the word. In our blindness we preferred its exact etymological opposite – the diabolic – that which tears apart.' Lindsay Clarke *The Chymical Wedding*
> Picador Edition 1990 : 160

In a previous chapter, I discussed the manner in which the 'kiss of the vampire' could disrupt things for the ancient Egyptians. Next, I want to think about the people or entities who do the attacking. To find them, we must come forward 1500 years to the time after the Pharaohs when Egypt was part of the Roman empire.

Contrary to what you might think, this is a very vibrant period for Egyptian religion. Yes, the Romans, and before them the Greeks, imposed harsh conditions that made it very hard for the traditional temple based religion to thrive. But kings and queens may come and go, these changes often have very less impact on the common people, the Rekhyt. The everyday religious liturgy may remain unchanged for millenia. However much the elite theology, the words may change, the underlying song often remains the same.

For instance, Egyptologists have discovered that some of the very oldest aspects of religion are found in its liturgy - songs, prayers and especially magical techniques. So for example, accounts from the classical world tell of the chanting in the Coptic churches and recall how it was much the same as was once heard in the 'pagan' temples. In other words, if you want to hear a faint echo of how Egyptian religion sounded, listen to the chanting of the Coptic church.

Most of what we know of the magick of this period comes from just one magician. His library was fortuitously uneathered in the early part of the nineteenth century and forms a substantial part of what is now known as the *Greek Magical Papyri*. We don't know his name, so to make this more user friendly I am going to call him 'Jeuy'. It is also possible that this magician was a woman. There is an increasing awareness of existence of female practitioners during this period. Male and female practitioners of the time share the same sobriquet - Hekaw - a little grammatical sign called a determinative tells us that they can be of either gender.[1]

Furthermore, to call this collection *Greek Magical Papyri* is a bit misleading, as a great many of the papyri are actually in the Egyptian language - but this is another of those elisions from the collective memory that accompanied the first European publication of this remarkable library.

If I may be allowed a digression here. The most famous text in the entire library is the Mithras Liturgi.[2] Entire books have been devoted to this text alone, and it has laid the basis for the modern reconstruction of the cult of Mithras. One of the principal sources was Franz Cumont's *Mysteries of Mithra*.[3] In a detailed chapter entitled

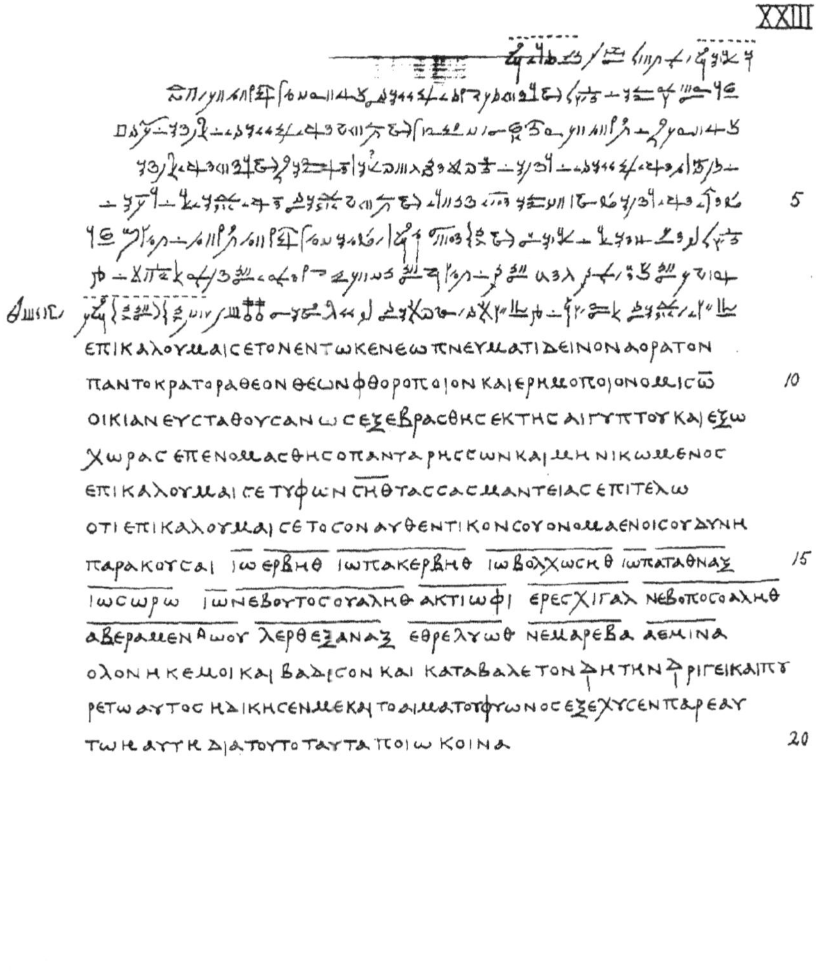

ΕΠΙΚΑΛΟΥΜΑΙϹΕΤΟΝΕΝΤΩΚΕΝΕΩΠΝΕΥΜΑΤΙΔΕΙΝΟΝΑΟΡΑΤΟΝ
ΠΑΝΤΟΚΡΑΤΟΡΑΘΕΟΝ ΘΕѠΝ ΦΘΟΡΟΠΟΙΟΝ ΚΑΙ ΕΡΗΜΟΠΟΙΟΝ ΟΜΙϹѠ
ΟΙΚΙΑΝ ΕΥϹΤΑΘΟΥϹΑΝ ѠϹ ΕΞΕΒΡΑϹΘΗϹ ΕΚ ΤΗϹ ΑΙΓΥΠΤΟΥ ΚΑΙ ΕΞѠ
ΧѠΡΑϹ ΕΠΕΝΟΜΑϹΘΗϹ Ο ΠΑΝΤΑ ΡΗϹϹѠΝ ΚΑΙ ΜΗ ΝΙΚѠΜΕΝΟϹ
ΕΠΙΚΑΛΟΥΜΑΙ ϹΕ ΤΥΦѠΝ ϹΗΘ ΤΑϹ ϹΑϹ ΜΑΝΤΕΙΑϹ ΕΠΙΤΕΛѠ
ΟΤΙ ΕΠΙΚΑΛΟΥΜΑΙ ϹΕ ΤΟ ϹΟΝ ΑΥΘΕΝΤΙΚΟΝ ϹΟΥ ΟΝΟΜΑ ΕΝ ΟΙϹ ΟΥ ΔΥΝΗ
ΠΑΡΑΚΟΥϹΑΙ ΙѠ ΕΡΒΗΘ ΙѠ ΠΑΚΕΡΒΗΘ ΙѠ ΒΟΛΧѠϹΗΘ ΙѠ ΠΑΤΑΘΝΑΞ
ΙѠϹѠΡѠ ΙѠ ΝΕΒΟΥΤΟϹ ΟΥΑΛΗΘ ΑΚΤΙѠΦΙ ΕΡΕϹΧΙΓΑΛ ΝΕΒΟΠΟϹΟΑΛΗΘ
ΑΒΕΡΑΜΕΝΘѠΟΥ ΛΕΡΘΕΞΑΝΑΞ ΕΘΡΕΛΥѠΘ ΝΕΜΑΡΕΒΑ ΑΕΜΙΝΑ
ΟΛΟΝ Η ΚΕΜΟΙ ΚΑΙ ΒΑΔΙϹΟΝ ΚΑΙ ΚΑΤΑΒΑΛΕ ΤΟΝ ΔΗ ΤΚΝ Δ ΡΙΓΕΙΚΑΙ ΠϹ
ΡΕΤѠ ΑΥΤΟϹ Η ΔΙΚΗϹΕΝ ΜΕΚΑΙ ΤΟ ΑΙΜΑ ΤΟΥ ΦѠΝΟϹ ΕΞΕΧΥϹΕΝ ΠΑΡ ΕΑΥ
ΤѠ Η ΑΥΤΗ ΔΙΑ ΤΟΥΤΟ ΤΑΥΤΑ ΠΟΙѠ ΚΟΙΝΑ

Figure 13: Papyrus London-Leiden 23/1-20. Now Papyrus Demotic Magical (PDM) xiv 675-94 [PGM xivc 15-27] in Betz (1986). This neatly written spell moves seamlessly between Egyptian and Greek. The overlining indicates words of particular significance - hence the Greek spelling 'Seth' is recognised whereas Greek 'Typhon' is recorded but not acknowledged as a genuine name of power.

'The Mithras Liturgy', Cumont tells us quite emphatically that women were forbidden from participating in the Romanised cult. Unfortunately, Cumont fails to also draw attention to the awkward fact that the Mithras Liturgy was written for a woman! The magician was initiating his own daughter or mystic sister into the cult. Perhaps, she had taken a fancy to Mithras, in a way similar to that of the modern chaos magician still might do. When you consider the implications of all this, does it make you think differently about Mithras? For me it serves to illustrate the dangers of making too many conservative assumptions about classical magick. Perhaps the magicians of the classical period were more radical than we realise, perhaps they were more like us than we previous imagined. The *Greek Magical Papyri* teach us to keep an open mind.

This magician (Jeuy) was a bilingual Egyptian priest based in Thebes. The collection is probably the record of Jeuy's 'study holiday' with the magi of Alexandria.[4] 'Study holiday' I hear you say, sounds a bit modern! Did people in the ancient world even have the concept of holidays? Well, as I have argued in several places now, it is probably best not to assume too much difference between us and them. Indeed, there were tourists in the ancient world. Many a pilgrim scratched his or her crude equivalent of 'I was here' and these graphiti can still be read on the walls of for example the Temple of Sety I at Abydos.

Through careful detective work, the eminent scholar Jacco Dielemann has reconstructed what little there is to be known about the life of the owner of the magical library. It is Dielemann who suggested the 'holiday' hypothesis for its first owner/author, who was an expert on Egyptian language and culture as well as fluent in Greek and several other vernaculars of his day. In the classical world there weren't too many people who had Jeuy's profile.

Life for the native Egyptian was fraught with difficulties - negotiating the apartheid system of their Greek rulers, then the painful transition to Roman domination and finally the growth of Christian fanaticism. Like many other libraries of this period it was hidden in the ground, in the hope of better times that never came. The owner never returned to claim his or her prize, perhaps he shared the fate of others of his kind, murdered at the hands of the mob. His library has been hidden for almost 2000 years, until humanity was again ready to receive its secrets - well almost. The contents are so revolutionary it has still not been completely published and remains largely unknown to the general public.

In chapter 1.1., I discussed an ancient spellkit found amongst the remains of the artisan village at Deir El Medina. I'll remind you that this is circa 1350BC. The spell kit enabled whoever possessed it to ward off the effects of 'evil sleep'[5] - repelling attacks of the 'evil dead'. Fourteen hundred years later and Egypt is under Roman rule, but the same magical techniques are still in vogue. Of the many hundreds of spells in the *Greek Magical Papyri* (PGM) several are for the sending of 'evil sleep'.

PDM xiv 675-94 [PGM XIVc 15-27]

The example I want to look at is written partly in Greek, partly in Demotic - the final form of the Egyptian language. This magician was seemlessly able to combine Egyptian mythology with native temple rituals in a very 'freeform' or improvised manner.

The rite was to be completed twice a day, at sunrise and sunset. It is repeated over four days causing the victim to suffer from evil sleep - 'nektek bin' (*nktk bin*).

If the process is continued for seven days, the victim would die (this later feature is written in code for obvious reasons).

The spell invokes Seth-Typhon to accomplish its aim using a technique known in the classical times as a diabolè - literally that which 'tears apart' as opposed to the symbolic - 'that which unites'. The appropriate god is provoked or antagonised even desecrated until he or she becomes sufficiently angry that they send a 'demonic' emissary to trouble the victim in their sleep.

Some modern practitioners impose an ethical frame on magick of this kind - maintaining a so-called 'threefold law of return' ie what you do rebounds on the doer threefold. Such a threefold law is not evident in classical magick. The magician hopes to remain immune from its effects. The kind of reverence for the gods we modern worshippers have is actually quite alien to Egyptian religion. The gods plague us, why shouldn't we plague them?

Instructions:
Spell to cause evil sleep

While facing the rising or setting sun, the practitioner should place

SUPERNATURAL ASSAULT IN ANCIENT EGYPT 151

Figure 14: Wooden Akh from Deir el-Medina, 1353-1336BCE - 18th Dynasty, reign of Akhenaten, Boston. Height 8cm

the head of a donkey between his feet and position his right *hand* in front of, and his left hand behind, the animal's head. While he is seated on his heels above the head, he has to recite the invocation. Before starting the rite, he has to anoint his right foot with yellow ochre from Syria, his left foot and soles with clay, and to put donkey's blood on one of his hands and the two corners of his mouth. As a phylactery, he should bind a thread of palm fibre to his hand and a piece of male palm fibre to the head and phallus. The accompanying Greek invocation runs as follows:

I call upon you who are in the empty air,
you who are terrible, invisible, almighty, a god of gods,
you who cause destruction and desolation,
you who hate a stable household,
you who were driven out of Egypt and have roamed foreign lands,
you who shatter everything and are not defeated.
I call upon you, Typhon Seth;
I command your prophetic powers because
I call upon your authoritative name,
to which you cannot refuse to listen,
then some barbarous names of power including:
IÔ erbÊth IÔ pakerbÊth IÔ bolchosÊth etc

Come to me and go and strike down him, NN, (or her, NN) with chills and fever. That very person has wronged me and he (or she) has spilled the blood of Typhon in his own (or her own) house. For this reason I am doing this (add the usual)

'The rite and the invocation are linked together through the

Egyptian god Seth, who was identified, at the latest from the fifth century BCE onwards, with the Greek deity Typhon, whom Zeus had punished for insurrection by throwing him into the Tartarus. The rite evokes a connection with Seth by means of the manipulation of the head and blood of a donkey, which animal was the symbol *par excellence* of the god Seth in Egyptian temple ritual throughout the Late and Greco-Roman period.'

Seth was/is one of the most important gods of ancient Egypt. Seth was the indigenous god whose cult was eclipsed by the new, perhaps foreign cult of Osiris in the early pre-dynastic times. The cult of Seth suffered a long decline until his only role remained as personification of 'evil' and murderer of the 'corn-king' Osiris. For a while under the Ramessides, Seth lost his negative character, becoming (once again) guardian of the spirit of monarchy. Seth continued to enjoy a secret life in Egypt, especially amongst Egypt's folk, the Rekhyt, traditionally where the 'old ways' tend to linger.

'To keep Seth's destructive powers ritually at bay, priests manipulated and destroyed small wax dolls or other inanimate objects as magical substitutes for Seth and his group of enemies in the daily temple ritual. However this spell to send evil sleep actually invokes the dangerous powers of Seth and, 'directs this destructive energy against a particular individual in a private matter.'

'The reversed nature of the present rite manifests itself most explicitly in the donkey's head. According to an account of Herodotus, Egyptian priests never offered an animal's head up to the god, but cursed it and took it outside the sacred precinct of the temple.

> After leading the marked beast to the altar where they [Egyptian priests] will sacrifice it, they kindle a fire; then they pour wine on the altar over the victim and call upon the god; then they cut its throat, and having done so sever the head from the body. They flay the carcass of the victim, then invoke many curses on its head, which they carry away. Where there is a market, and Greek traders in it, the head is taken to the market and sold; where there are no Greeks, it is thrown into the river. The imprecation, which they utter over the heads, is that whatever ill threatens those who sacrifice, or the whole of Egypt, fall upon that head. In respect of the heads of sacrificed beasts and the libation of wine, the practice of all Egyptians is the same in all sacrifices; and from this ordinance no Egyptian will taste of the head of anything that had life.
> [Herodotus, *The Histories*, II, 39]

Therefore, by making use of the head of a donkey, the rite does not only establish a close relationship with Seth, but also it defines itself as a rite opposed to the rules of regular temple ritual, which is in accord with Seth's role as enemy to the ordered world. When the practitioner applies the donkey's blood to one of his hands, he trespasses in the same way another rule of Egyptian temple ritual. Since blood was seen as impure, the flowing of the sacrificial victim's blood symbolized the triumph over the enemies in regular temple ritual. In this particular case, the practitioner does not cast the blood

Figure 15: Larger anthropoid bust representing the *Akh* - from Museum Fine Arts, Boston. Height: 24cm

away, but smears it on his hand and, in the act, identifies with the enemies by way of contiguity.

'Next to Seth, the rite is also concerned with the sun god Ra, since the invocation has to be recited to the sun, while the practitioner faces the rising and setting sun disk. Daybreak and evening were probably considered opportune moments for this rite, because they are the beginning and end of the sun god's nightly travel through the underworld, where he has to enter into battle with the forces of chaos and evil, who attempt to bring the sun boat to a standstill in their effort to subdue the forces of creation and rejuvenation. By reciting at these critical moments between light and darkness, the practitioner takes full advantage of the intensified activity of the forces of disorder. More-over, according to pharaonic sun theology, the god Seth, part of the sun boat's crew as a servant to Re, exerted his destructive powers now to combat the snake Apophis, the sun god's arch-rival in the underworld. Seth and the sun god were consequently believed to be in each other's presence at these moments.'

The Greek invocation develops the Sethian elements of the rite further by calling the deity the god of cosmic upheaval, who is hostile to the social order and dwells in foreign countries. As outsider to the divine pantheon, the social world and the land Egypt, he is the appropriate candidate to take up the anti-social task. In the final lines of the invocation, the practitioner prompts the deity to come to his aid by accusing the victim of having 'spilled the blood of Typhon in his own (or her own) house' (line 19-20).' [6]

In the unlikely eventuality of someone wanting to reconstruct the above ritual for themselves, either in whole or part, the previous five chapters give more than enough information. Perhaps this is a slightly downbeat note on which to end; with all this talk of 'evil sleep.' But as the ancients knew only too well, in the right hands, even a poison can become a therapy. I am offering another piece in the very complex jigsaw that is the god Seth, whose mysteries we know by negating the negation.

Notes

1. Edwards I ES (1960) *Hieratic Papyri In the British Museum, 4th series - Amuletic Decrees*, BM L1
2. Betz, H D (ed) (1986) *The Greek Magical Papyri in Translation*, Chicago. Betz has also written a monograph on PGM IV 475 - 829 (Mithras Liturgy)
3. Cumont, Franz (1903) *Mysteries of Mithra*, translated by T J McCormack, Kegan Paul. See page 173 for supposed interdiction against women.
4. Dieleman, Jacco (2005) *Priests, Tongues and Rites - the London-Leiden Magical Manuscripts and Translation in Egyptian Ritual* (100-300CE), Brill.
5. NKTK BN in Demotic. NKTK meaning sleep, which I would say was a synonym for the evil dreams discussed at length in Szpakowska, Kasia (2003) *Behind Closed Eyes: dreams and nightmares in Ancient Egypt*, Wales. The most commonly used word for dream was rsw.t, a noun with no verbal form - signifying that a dream was a concrete vision rather than an activity of the sleeper.
6. Dieleman, *op cit*, pp130-135

Bibliography

Abbreviations:

BSAK Beiheft Studien zur Altägyptischa Kulture.

EES: Egyptian Exploration Society

JARCE: Journal of the American Research Center in Egypt.

JEA: Journal of Egyptian Archaeology

JEOL: Jaarbericht van het Vooraziatrich Egyptisch Genootschap (Gezelschap) "Ex Orient Lux"

JJP: Journal of Juristic Papyrology

Lexikon: Lexikon de Ägyptologie (six vols) ed. Wolfgang Helck, Eberhard Otto, and Wolfhart Westendorf (Wiesbaden: O. Harrassowitz, 1972).

OMRU: Oudheidkundige Mededelingen Uit Het Rijks Museum ca Oudheden re Leiden.

RDeE: Revue d'Égyptology, Le Caire.

SAK = Studien zur Altägyptischa Kulture

Urk: Urkenden des ägyptischen Altertums; see Steindorff, G (1903)

Books

Allen, James P (1994) 'Reading a Pyramid' in *Homages à Jean Leclant*, Vol I pp. 5-28. Inst Français d'Archéologie Orientale.

Allen, James P (2005) 'The Art of Medicine in Ancient Egypt: an exhibition at the Metropolitan Museum of Art' *KMT* Vol 16 No 3 Fall edition, pp 43-47

Andrews, Carol AR (1995) 'An unusual source for magical texts' in *Studies in Ancient Egypt in honour of H S Smith*, EES pp.11-16.

Assmann, Jan (2001) *The Search for God in Ancient Egypt*, translated by David Lorton, Cornell.

Bác, Tamás A (1987) 'Prolegomena to the study of Calendars of Lucky and Unlucky days.' in Roccati A,.& A Siliotti *La Magia in Egitto ai Temple dei Faraoni*.

Baines, J (1990) 'Residual Knowledge, Hierarchy and Decorum' *JARCE* 27, pp1.22. Good overview of the issue of initiation

Baines, J & Malek, J, (2000) *Cultural Atlas of Ancient Egypt*, Andromeda

Bakir, A M, (1966) *The Cairo Calendar*, Cairo

Betz, H D (ed) (1986) *The Greek Magical Papyri in Translation*, Chicago.

Billigmeier, Jon-Christian (!987) 'Alphabets', entry in *Encyclopedia of Religions*, edited by Mircea Eliade, New York.

Bika Reed, (1987) *Rebel in the Soul*: translation of Berlin Papyrus 3023, Vermont.

Blackman, A. M. and H W Fairman (1943) 'The Myth of Horus at Edfu II', *JEA* 29.

Borchardt, L (1935) *Die Mittel zur zeitlichen Festiegung von Punkten der ägyptische Geshichte und ihre anwerdung.*

Borghouts, J (1987) 'Akhu and Hekau' in *La Magia in Egitto ai Temple dei Faraoni*, ed Roccati A & A Siliotti

Boylan, P (1922) *Thoth, the Hermes of Egypt*, OUP.

Breasted, James H (1906) *Ancient Records of Egypt*, 5 vols, Chicago.

Brewer, Douglas & Friedman, R F (1989) *Fish and Fishing in Ancient Egypt*, Aris & Philips, UK.

Brugsch, Heinrich (1883) *Thesaurus Inscriptionum Aegyptiacarum*, 6 vols Leipzig.

Brugsch Heinrich (1891) *Die Aegyptolgie*, Leipzig.

Budge, E A Wallis (1901) *The Book of the Dead*, Kegan Paul.

Budge, E A Wallis (1906) *Egyptian Heaven & Hell*, Vol II, 'Book of Gates'.

Budge, E A Wallis (1923) *Hieratic Papyri in the British Museum*, 1st series. Contents: Festival Songs of Isis and Nephthys; Litanies of Sokar; Book of Overcoming Apep, Harris Magical Papyrus, Calendar of Lucky & Unlucky days.

Budge, E A Wallis (1923) *Hieratic Papyri in the British Museum*, 2nd series including Papyrus Sallier, British Museum

Cerny, J (1943) 'The meaning of Tyby', *Annales du Science des Antiquities* 43, pp173-181

Cheke, Aaron (2004) 'Magic through the linguistic lenses of Greek mágos, Indo-European *mag(h)-, Sanskrit màyà and Pharaonic Egyptian ¡eka' in *Journal for the Academic Study of Magic II*, Mandrake of Oxford.

Collier Mark & B Manley (1998) *How to Read Egyptian Hieroglyphs*, BM London.

Clarke, John R (2003) *Roman Sex,* New York, Abrams.

Clagett, M (1995) *Ancient Egyptian Science II, Calendars, Clocks and Astronomy*, American Philosophical Society.

Darby, William (1977), Paul Ghalounqui & Louis Grivetti, *Food - The Gift of Osiris*, 2 vols London.

David, Antony E & Rosalie (1992) *A Biographical Dictionary of Ancient Egypt*, London.

Demarée, Robert J. (1983) *The 3ḫ ikr n Ra Stelae. On Ancestor Worship in Ancient Egypt*, Leiden.

Depuydt, L (1998) 'Hieroglyphic representation of the moon's absence' (*psḏntyw*) in *Festschrift W A Ward*.

Depuydt, L (1997) *Civil Calendar and Lunar Calendar in Ancient Egypt*, Leuven.

Depuydt, L (1999) *Fundamentals of Egyptian Grammar*, Frog Publishing, Massachusetts.

Derchain, Philippe (1962) *La Lune: mythes and rites*, Sources Orientales, Edition de Seuil, Paris.

Dieleman, Jacco (2005) *Priests, Tongues and Rites - the London-Leiden Magical Manuscripts and Translation in Egyptian Ritual* (100-300CE), Brill.

Doblhofer, E (1961) *Voices in Stone: The Decipherment of Ancient Scripts and Writing*, Souvenir.

Dornseiff, Franz (1925) *Das Alphabet in Mystik und Magie*, Berlin

Draco, Melusine (2001) *The Egyptian Book of Days - Calendars of Ancient Egypt*, Ignatus.

Draco, Melusine (2003) *The Egyptian Book of Nights* (zodiacs)

Duell, Prentice (1938) *The Mastaba of Mereruka*, 2 Vols, Chicago.

Edmonds, Radcliffe G III (??) 'At the Seizure of the Moon: the absence of the moon in the Mithras Liturgy' in *Prayer, Magick, and the Stars in the Ancient and Late Antique World*, Edited by Noegel, Walker & Wheeler, Pennsylvania State University Press.

Edwards, I E S (1950) *Oracular Amuletic Decrees of the Late New Kingdom*, 2 vols, Hieratic Papyris in the British Museum 4th series.

Emboden, William (1989) 'The Sacred Journey in Dynastic Egypt: Shamanistic Trance in the Context of the Narcotic Water Lily and the Mandrake, *Journal of Psychoactive Drugs* Vol 21(I) Jan-Mar pp 61-75.

Evans, L (2001) *Kingdom of the Ark*, Simon & Schuster.

Faulkner, (1956) *JEA* 42, text of *Berlin Pap 3024*.

Forbes, D C (2005) 'Set, Lord of Chaos' *KMT*, Vol 15 No 4 pp 67-71

Frankfurter, David (1998) *Religion in Roman Egypt*,

Frankfurter, David (1994) 'The Magic of writing and the writing of magic. The power of the word in Egyptian and Greek tradition.' *Helios* 21 (1924) pp.189 - 221, 199-205.

Fries, J (1992) *Visual Magick: A Handbook of Freestyle Shamanism*, Mandrake of Oxford.

Fries, J (2004) *Cauldron of the Gods: A Manual of Celtic Magick*, Mandrake of Oxford.

Fries, J (2005) *Helrunar: a Manual of Rune Magick*, Mandrake of Oxford.

Gardiner A H (1917) 'Professional Magicians in Egypt', *Proceedings of the Society for Biblical Archaeology 19*.

Gardiner, A H & K Sethe (1928) *Egyptian Letters to the Dead - mainly from the Middle Kingdom, copied, translated and edited*, EES.

Gardiner, A H (1931) *Chester Beatty Papyrus I*, Oxford University Press.

Gardiner A H (1938) 'The House of Life', JEA 24, 157-79pp.

Gardiner, A H (1941-48) *The Wilbour Papyrus*, 3 Vols, Oxford.

Gardiner, A H (1944) 'Horus the Behdetite' *JEA* 30 pp24ff.

Gardiner, A H (1947) *Ancient Egyptian Onomastica*, OUP.

Gardiner, AH (1950) 'The Baptism of Pharoah' *JEA* 36 pp3-12.

Gardiner A H (1955) *The Ramesseum Papyri*, OUP.

Gardiner, A H (1957) *Egyptian Grammar: being an introduction to the study of Hieroglyphs*, 3rd revised edition, Oxford.

Gasse, A (2004) 'Une Stèle d'horus sur les crocodiles à propos du <text C>' *Revue D'Égyptologie*, tome 55, pp23-44.

Gaster, Theodor H (1961) *Thespis: ritual, myth and drama in the ancient Near East*, New York.

Gautier J E & Jéquier, G (1902) *Fouilles de Licht*, L'Institute Français D'Archeologie Oriental, Vol 6.

Ginzel K F (1906) *Handbuch de Mathematischen und technischen chronologie*, Leipzig

Griffiths, J G (1960) *The Conflict of Horus and Seth*, Liverpool.

Gupta, S, Hoens, D K & Goudriaan T (1979) *Hindu Tantrism*, Leiden.

Harer W Benson (1985) 'Pharmacological and Biological Properties of the Egyptian Lotus' Hayes, JARCE XXII pp49-54

Herodotus, Translation by A D Godley, Loeb Classical Library

Hikade, Thomas (2003) 'Getting the ritual right - fishtale knives in predynastic Egypt' pp 137-152 in *Egypt - Temple of the Whole World - Studies in Honour of Jan Assmann*, Brill.

Hutton, R (1999) *The Triumph of the Moon: a history of modern pagan witchcraft*, OUP.

Kaper, O (1995 'The astronomical ceiling of Deir el Haggar in the Dakhla Oasis' JEA 81 151-73.

Katzeff, Paul (1990) *Moon Madness and other effects of the Full Moon*, Hale.

Kees, Herman (1923-4) *Horus and Seth als Götterpaar*, Göttingen

Kees, Hermann (1977) *Ancient Egypt*, Chicago UP.

Koefoed-Petersen, O, (1948) *Les Stèles Égyptiennes,* Copenhagen.

Kloetzli, R W (1985) 'Maps of Time - Mythologies of Descent: Scientific Instruments and the Cosmograph' *History of Religions* 25 pp. 120-45.

Lajtar, A (1991) 'Proskynema - inscriptions of a corporation of Iron workers from Hermonthis in the temple of Hatshepsut in Deir el-Bahari; new evidence of Pagan cults in the 4th century ad', *Journal of Juristic Papyrology* 21 (1991) 53-70

Legge, F (1905) 'Magic Ivories of the Middle Kingdom' Proceedings of the Society of Biblical Archaeology, pp 130-152 + plates.

Leibovitch, J, (1943-45) 'Le griffon' parts I, II & III, *Bulletin de l'Institut d'Égypte, Le Caire.,* Nos., 25, 26 & 27.

Lexikon de Ägyptologie (six vols) ed. Wolfgang Helck, Eberhard Otto, and Wolfhart Westendorf (Wiesbaden: O. Harrassowitz, 1972)

Leiris, Michel (1958) *La Possession et ses aspects théatraux chez le Ethipeins de Gondar,* Paris

Lewis, I M (1971) *Ecstatic Religion*, Penguin books.

Messing, Simon (1958) 'Group therapy and social sta tus in the Zar cult of Ethiopia' *American Anthropologist* 60 pp 1120-7.

Lichtheim, Miriam (1980) *Ancient Egyptian Literature*, 3 vols, University of California Press.

Littmann, Enno (1950) *Arabische Geisterbeschwörungen aus Ägypten*, Harrassowitz Verlag, Leipzig

Logan, JJ (1990) 'The Origins of the Jmy-wt fetish', *JARCE* 27, pp 61-70

Luft, Ulruch (1986) Götitnger Miszellen 92 for feast dates

Mercer, S A B (1949) *The Religion of Ancient Egypt*, London, London, Luzac 1949).

Metcalf P & Huntington, W R (1979) *Celebrations of Death*, CUP NY

Morgan, M (2005) *Tankhem, Seth and Egyptian Magick*, Mandrake of Oxford.

Morgan, C (2002) *Medicine of the Gods: basic principles of Ayurvedic medicine*, Mandrake.

Morgan, M (2006) *The Bull of Ombos: Seth and Egyptian magick II*, Mandrake.

Nabarz, Payam (2005) *The Mysteries of Mithras: The Pagan Belief That Shaped the Christian World*, USA.

Neugebauer O (1949) 'The Early History of the Astrolabe' *Isis* 40, pp.240-256.

Neugebauer O & Parker, R (1962) Ancient Egyptian Astronomical Texts, 4 vols, Brown University.
I. Early Decans
II. Ramesside Star Clocks
III. Decans, Planets, Constellations & Zodiacs
IV. Plates.

Nicholson P T & Shaw I, (2000) *Ancient Egyptian Materials and Technology*, Cambridge.

Nilsson, Martin P (1920) *Primitive Time Reckoning* , Lund.

Parker, Richard A (1950) *The Calendars of Ancient Egypt*, Chicago.

Parker, Richard A (1959) *Vienna Demotic Papyri on Luna Omina*, Brown University.

Parker, Richard A (1962) *A Saite Oracle Papyrus from Thebes (Papyrus Brooklyn 47.218.3)* Brown University

Pinch, Geraldine (1994) *Magic in Ancient Egypt*, British Museum Press.

Plutarch, *On Isis and Osiris,* Greek with English translation by Gwyn Griffiths, Cardiff.

Preisendanz, Karl (1928 & 1931) *Papyri Graecae Magicae*, 2 Vols, Leipzig. Reprinted Stuttgart 1973-4)

Ghalioungui, P (1965) Magic & Medical Science in Anceint Egypt, Hodder & Stoughton.

Reiner, Erica (1975-), with David Pingree, *Babylonian Planetary Omens*, (The Enuma Anu Enlil) Brill/Styx.
Vol II Fasc 1 Venus Tablet of Ammisaduga (1975)
Vol II Fasc 2 Constellations (1981)
Vol III: Venus Omens (1998)
Vol IV: Jupiter Omens (2005)

Reymond, E A E (1969) *The Mythological Origin of the Egyptian Temple*, Manchester University Press.

Ritner, R K (1990) 'Ostracon Gardiner 363 - a spell against night terrors.' *JARCE* 27 25-41.

Ritner, R K (1993) *The Mechanics of Ancient Egyptian Magical Practice*, Chicago.

Ritner, R K (1996) 'Dream Oracles' in Hallo, William W, *The Context of Scripture* Vol I, Brill.

Rose, Lyne (1999) *Sun, Moon & Sothis: a study of calendars & calendar reforms in Ancient Egypt*.

Samuel D & Bolt P (1995) 'Rediscovering Ancient Egyptian Beer', *Brewer's Guardian UK*, December pp27-32.

Schott, S (1950) *Altägyptische Festdaten*, Wiesbaden.

Servajean, F (2004) 'Lune ou Soleil d'or un Épisode des aventures 'Horus et de Seth (P Chester Beatty I R° 11 1-13 1)' *Revue D'Égyptologie*, Tome 55, pp125-148.

Shaw, Ian (1995) *Dictionary of Ancient Egypt*, BM. 'priest'

Shorter, Alan W (1935), 'The God Nehebkau', JEA XXi pp47sq

Spalinger, A (1991) 'An unexpected source in a festival calendar' RdeE 41.

Spalinger, A (1992) *Three Studies of Egyptian Feasts and their chronological implications* - Baltimore, USA.

Spalinger, A (1993) 'A chronological analysis of the feast of *thy*' *Studien Zur Altägyptischer Culture* 20, pp289-303.

Spalinger, A (1994) *Revolutions in Time: Studies in Ancient Egyptian Calendrics*, Van Siclen Books, Texas.

Stadelmann, R (1967) *Syrisch-palästinensische Gottheiten in Ägypten*, Leiden.

Te Velde (1967) *Seth: God of Confusion: a study of his role in Egyptian Mythology and Religion*, E J Brill (rev 1977).

Te Velde (1970) 'The God Heka in Egyptian Theology' *JEOL* 21 175-186 followed by unnumbered plate section.

Troy, L (1987) 'Have a nice day!' in *The Religion of the Ancient Egyptians - Cognitive Structures*, Proceedings of Symposia in Uppsala & Bergen (ed) Englund, G, pp.127 [316 Upp].

Versnel, H. S.(2002) 'The Poetics of the Magical Charm : An Essay on the Power of Words.' In *Magic and Ritual in the Ancient World*, edited by Paul Allan Mirecki and Marvin W. Meyer, 105-58. Leiden: E. J. Brill, 2002.

Vernus, (1981), 'Omina Calendérique et comptabilité d'offrandes sur une tablette Hiératique de la XVIIIe Dynastie' RdeE, vol 33 pp89-124.Pap Leyden I 346.

Van Walsen (1982) 'Month names and feast at Deir el-Medina' in *Gleanings from Deir el-Medina* eds Memaree & Janssen, pp. 214-46, Leiden.

Von Bomhard, Anne-Sophie *The Egyptian Calendar*, Periplus 1999.

Wainwright, G A (1923) 'The Red Crown in Early prehistoric times', *JEA* 9, pp26-33.

Wainwright, G A (1938) *The Sky Religion in Egypt: its antiquity and effects*, Cambridge.

Wainwright, G A (1932) 'Letopolis', *JEA 19* pp. 164-167

Wainwright, G A (1935), 'Celestial Associations of Min', *JEA* 21 pp.152-170.

Wells, R A (1985) 'The Satet Temple on Elephantine: an Egyptian Stonehenge' SAK 12 pp274

Wells, R A (1990) 'Ra and the Calendars', in Spalinger (1994).

Glossary

Acacia: tree associated with Seth and Osiris. An artifact in the Metropolitan Museum of Art shows Tawaret (Hippo), together with Mut (Mother) emerging from an Acacia. The seed pods have an astringent, antibacteriological properties and were used in Egyptian medicine for uterine complaints and infections. (see Allen J P 2005)

Acrophany: a particular sound is expressed by means of a common Egyptian word of which only the first consonant has phonetic relevance. (Dielemann 2005 : 78)

Alexandrian calendar has an additional epagomenal day every four years to arrest the forward shift of dates.

Amon: originally a wind deity, who rises in Ramesside theology, to be, together with Ra, King of the Gods, much as in later hermetic theology, the 'pantocrator' stands above the 'lesser' gods. Prototype is represented as a human being (at times ithyphallic), wearing a mortarboard crowned with two plumes or, at times, with a ram's head, the animal dedicated to him. With the goddess Mut and the god Khonsu, they formed the Theban Triad. He was also identified with the god Ra and venerated under the name of Amon-Ra. The cult's principal location was in Thebes.

Anath: Canaanite-Phoenician goddess of fertility and victory

Ankh-tawi: Necropolis near Memphis, Ptah, south-of-his-wall was lord of Ankhtawy, Bast was called Lady of Ankhtawy

Anubis: a jackal-headed god who presided over mummification and accompanied the dead to the hereafter.

Apep, Apophis, demon of non-being, the opponent of Ra. His

companions referred to as the 'children of Bedesh' and 'children of the storm' in Cairo Calendar

Astarte: Canaanite goddess, called *Lady of Heaven* by the Egyptians.

Atef: the double-feathered crown of Osiris

Ba: 'soul' – after death, the person live on in this form not on earth but in the tomb and the community's memory. Ba is the characteristic manifestation of a entiry, divine or human. Bears comparison with Hindu: 'Linga'.

Banebdjedet: Ram-headed primeval deity of Djedet (Mendes).

Barque of the Millions of Years: Ra's Manjet boat, with which he sailed through the 12 provinces of the day. For his night journeys, Ra used his Mesket boat.

Bebon (*b3b3wj*) also Baba:.Baboon god and demon of sexual potency and prowess with red ears and features of Seth. Names in various texts including Plutarch and Almanacs of Lucky & Unlucky Days. See Kees, Horus & Seth II 47-48

Bousiris: from the Egyptian, meaning 'City of Osiris'. A city in Lower Egypt where the worship of Osiris was born.

Canopic urns: four urns contained the liver, lungs, stomach and intestines extracted from the body during mummification.

Castles for millions of years: On the west bank of the Nile at Thebes, the Pharaohs of the 18th, 19th and 20th Dynasties had large religious monuments built, which were improperly called 'funerary temples'. In reality, they used them, during their liftime, to worship the deified pharaoh associated with Amon, the main Theban deity.

Chaîne Opératoire - methological concept devised in the 1960s by André Leroi-Gourhan in which the sequence of construction and deconstruction is analysed for information about the culture behind an artefact.

Cheth = CTh or Seth in etc. A secret name of power.

Cippus: Latin term meaning post or stake. In archaeology: 'a small low column, sometimes without a base or capital and most frequently bearing an inscription.' (OED: Gwily, J ,1842, An Encyclopedia of Architecture: historical, theoretic and practical.) Used in Egyptology in reference to the Horus 'Cippi' - an image of 'Horus among the crocodiles.' The inscription describes an episode whereby Isis, during their sojourn in the Delta marshes hiding from Seth, cures the infant Horus of the effects of scorpion bite. Water collected in these Cippi is considered magically potent to ward off the effects of scorpion stings.

Coffin Texts: a term reserved for those spells which are peculiar to the early coffins and do not recur later, not at least until the Saite period, when some of them were sporadically revived. These Coffin Texts contain excerpts from the earliest Pyramid Texts, usurped by the nobility of the IX-XI dynasties for their own benefit (Gardiner: 1927:13).

Critical edition: a special edition of a text, edited from several sources to produce a final scholarly edition. This so-called 'critical edition' may not correspond with any of the extant 'street' editions of a text, and for this reason is viewed by some as a distortion.

Cubit: approximately half a metre

Damanhur: 'Town of Horus', argued by some to be the original Behadit in the western delta, until its transfer to Edfu as the 'Behadit' of Upper Egypt.

Dead (western): the Land of the Setting Sun: this is the Kingdom of the Dead.

Dendara: the capital of the sixth Nome of Upper Egypt, and its necropolis contains tombs dug between the predynastic period and the end of the Old Kingdom. This site's renown is due to the famous Temple of Hathor, which dates back to the Greco-Roman period. Dendara was dedicated to Hathor, one of the oldest Egyptian deities, represented as a cow or a woman with cow's ears.

Djed: a pillar, symbol of stability and duration; it represents Osiris' spinal column. It is also a protective amulet.

Decan: 36 stars on the belt of the southern ecliptic, whose rising was used to mark the passage of the 'hours' during each cycle or 'week' of ten days.

Ears, smashing of. A rite connected with Bata* - See Cairo Calendar

Egyptian: A language of the Hamiti-Semitic group which includes Semitic, Berber, Cushitic and Hausa)

Epagomenal: see Intercalary.

Ennead: (*psdt*) 'The company of heaven', 'companions of the sun & moon', A group of more or less nine deities, such as the company of *Heliopolis* - Atum, Shu and Tefnut, Geb and Nut, Osiris and Isis, Seth, Nephthys.

Êsenephus = *s.t-nb.t ḥw.t* = Isis & Nephthys - in 'garbled' version of PGM

Griffin: The griffin is an important avatar of Seth appearing on talismanic wands made from hippo ivory - the name is 'teshtesh' in Middle Egyptian. Leibovitch once remarked: 'that as "dieu sauveur" Seth is a griffin. On the one hand the griffin is a guardian angel, on the other an avenger, pursuing its enemies at furious speed or crushing them underfoot, as appears from the many illustrations in the articles by Leibovitch. It might be that at Beni Hasan these two functions are divided over the falcon-headed griffin and the Seth-animal, and that the occurrence of griffins with a falcon's head or the head of the Seth-animal is not altogether arbitrary, but is connected with the duality of the gods Horus and Seth in mythology.' J. Leibovitch, *Le griffon I*, *BIE* 25 (1943), p. 188 and fig. 5 quoted in Te Velde.

Harpoon: the main weapons used for hunting hippos.

Head: 'reserve', a substitute for the mummy's head, placed in the tomb of the deceased in case the latter is destroyed (see Hayes 1953 : 109).

Histeriola: divine precedent for a spell.

Hathor: cow-headed deity (sometimes depicted as a woman with cow's ears) protected women and the dead, as she was likened to the Goddess of the Kingdom of the Dead; she was also goddess of music and intoxication.

Horus: god of the sky and protector of the pharaoh to whom he was likened. Horus could be depicted as a falcon-headed man. As the son of Osiris and Isis, he was often represented as infant (Harpocrates) with a finger held to his lips; a gesture rather paradoxically interpreted in the Hermetic Order of the Golden Dawn, as 'the sign of silence.'

Iathath = (ie Seth). In the Greek Magical Papyrus (Betz 1986). The black 'blood' of Seth.

Ideogramme: a pictorial sign, that has no phonetic value but nevertheless helps define the meaning or sense rather than the sound of a word. Incidentally where the ideogramme follows one or more phonogrammes and ends the word, it is known as a determinative. The ideogrammes are historically the oldest part of the Egyptian language, the phonograms later prefixed to it for the sake of clarity (Gardiner 1926).

Intercalary: twelve lunar months of 30 days equals 360, which leaves five extra or intercalary days, on which the priests of Heliopolis assigned the birth of five gods, almost as a supplement to their own theological system. The five gods said to be born on these days were: Osiris, Isis, Seth, Nephthys and Horus the child. This schema is known from Pyramid Text 1961 and Plutarch, *Isis and Osiris*, 12. Mercer (1949 : 277) states that the priests of Heliopolis had invented this calendar by 2781BC.

Ipet Hemet: Hippo or perhaps Hathor?

Jeu, Books of and Jeu the Hieroglyphist of the so-called 'Headless One' ritual of PGM (known in contemporary magick variously as the 'Bornless One', 'Liber Samech' and 'Preliminary Invocation of the Goetia') . *The Books of Jeu* are Coptic / Gnostic texts found at Nag Hammadi.

Kiki: seemingly the burning oil from the castor oil plant (ricinus communis) used in lamps.

Khmun: Hermopolis Magna in Middle Egypt, cult centre of Thoth.

Ladder of Seth: means by which the king's soul rises to the stars. Made of iron that has fallen from the heavens. Jacob's ladder may also be a meteorite (see Wainwright).

LPH: abreviation used by Egyptologists for stative formula: 'Life, Prosperity and Health' - *$ꜥnḥ(w)$ $wḏꜣ(w)$ $snb(w)$* - 'alive, sound and healthy' or 'Life, prosperity and health' in older translations.

Lucky/Unlucky days. There are several surviving examples of these 'calendars' of lucky and unlucky days. Calendar is misleading as they are closer to almanacs than true calendars. They do contain some crucial local traditions although often omit welknown local feast days such as *W3g*.

Maat heru: speaking true, which will get you through the gates after judgement.

Maat: divine personification of the cosmic order, secondarily connected to the concepts of truth and justice. She wears an ostrich plume on her head, the transcription of her name.

Min: in origin a sky god - one of whose forms is as a white bull tethered to axial pillar as cult object.

Mut: the wife of Amon, she was venerated in Thebes. Originally depicted as a vulture, she later took on a human form.

Neolithic: of or relating to the cultural period of the Stone Age beginning around 10,000BC in the Middle East and later elsewhere, characterized by the development of agriculture and the making of polished stone implements.

Neter: god or the divine.

Nehes: Nubia; (later Kash: Kush), according to Baynes & Malek (2000) the derivation of 'Nubia' may be from 'Nub' - meaning gold.

Neith: goddess of the hunt and war, whose cult centre was at Sais.

Nome: one of forty-two administrative districts, significantly also the number of the judges of the dead. Interestingly each Nome coincides with one of the enormous temporary lakes caused by the annual Nile flood (Butzer 1976).

Nomen: the King's titulary consisted of five great names. The family name, called the nomen by Egyptologists, is introduced by epithet 'son of Ra'.

On: Heliopolis

Onnophris: Osiris as known in the tradition of the magical papyri and Christianity, about whom is said: He brings peace to the lands in his name of Sokaris, mighty is his reputation in his name of Osiris, he persists until the ends of eternity in his name Onnophris.

Onomastica: words lists detailing divinity and geography. See final book of Apuleus' *Golden Ass* for an example, where it says her true name only known to the Egyptians and Ethiopians.

Onuris: Anhur, god of hunt and war, resident at This. He returns the Eye of the Sun as his consort Mehit.

Osiris: the husband of Isis; after having been killed by his brother, Seth, he fathered a son, Horus, who, grown to adulthood, avenged him. He is represented with his crown (atef), his scepter (bequa), and his flail, (nekhekh).

Pronomen: King's first cartouche or throne name.

Palaeolithic: of or relating to the cultural period of the Stone Age beginning with the earliest chipped stone tools, about 750,000 years ago, (incidentally same time as the Nile found its way out of Africa) until the beginning of the Mesolithic Age, about 15,000 years ago.

Peganum harmala see 'Ruin Weed'.

Pars pro toto: 'part stands for the whole'. Ie type of time reckoning based on the observation of a single event to represent the whole cycle. For example the Slavonic *Leto* means the 'summer' and 'year'. It may seem obvious to us in temperate climes that there is only one summer per year, and therefore we could say 'she is a maid of eighteen summers' and we would all understand that.. But in some equatorial regions there is no winter or summer and there are two wet seasons! Some old traditions ignore or lump together whole segments of the year - hence the old Roman year of ten months.

Petosis: an Hellenistic astrologer who made an association between the Northern Constellations and the Lunar days. Source: Neugebauer & Parker (1962 III : 216). Most reference books say this Petosis is the occupant of the famous Hermopolitan 4th century BC tomb, but N&P cast doubt on this and indeed the theories of Petosis. The late text to which they refer is not quoted in their monumental work but may be in Neugebauer's 'Egyptian Planetary Texts' *Transactions of the American Philosophical Society*, Vol XXXII part II, Jan 1942 209-50.

PDM = Papyri Demotika Magicae

PGM = Papyri Graecae Magicae – Preisendanz's (qv) sobriquet, although he omitted the Demotic spells as of less interest and therefore ensured they disappeared from scholarly discourse for the best part of a century.

Pharaoh: Egyptian word for king is 'nsw' - 'pharaoh', as used in the Hebrew Bible is probably derived from 'per'o' - king's house.

Pluvial: a rainy period or age.

Preisendanz, Karl, editor of the PGM in two volumes, 1928 & 1931.

Pre-Harakhti: a combination of Re and Horus!

Ptah: the God of Memphis, brought the universe into being along with the hieroglyphic pictogrammes, the most primitive level of the Egyptian language. These were later simplified and reduced to a short list of alphabetic signs by Thoth, the god of scribes. Ptah, the husband of the Lion Goddess, Sekhmet, was depicted wearing a mummy's shroud, holding in his hand a scepter. He was later likened to another Memphis god of death, Sokaris, and was worshipped in his syncretic form of Ptah-Sokaris.

Pawet (*p3wt*): a cake connected with the rites of Hathor.

Pylon: a monumental temple entrance, consisting of a portal between two enormous trapezoidal monoliths.

Ra, or Re, as Egyptian sun-god Ra. Ra was beholden to Seth for defending him against the demons who assailed him on his daily journey through the skies.

Rekhyt: the plebs, others say the followers of Seth

Ruin Weed: So named because commonly found on archeaological sites in the Middle East. Latin name Peganum harmala, also known as *Telepathine*.

Sais: centre in western delta, where local rulers, decendents of 25th dynasty, became important in the conflicts of the 8th century BCE.

Sekhem: 'power', 'sign of power' hence 'image' or 'statue'. The Ba (qv) returns or is installed in the mummy / corpse / statue giving power. Assmann discussed this in relation to the hermetic doctrine 'as above, so below'.

Sekhmet: lion-headed goddess, sometimes crowned with the

solar disk. She protected the royal power; she can be likened to Hathor, Bastet and Isis.

Setna, Khamuas: Khaemwase, son of Ramesses II and Isis-Nefert. He died in the 55th year of the reign of his father. He was sem-priest of Ptah and chief artificer. Setme: also Setna - sem, the title of Khaemwase

Sw: a town of Seth, mentioned in *Cairo Calendar*

Shed: 'save', 'rescue', 'saviour' - used especially after the traumas of the Amarna period. The Egyptian aspect of the semitic god Reshef - or young saviour god used as an epithet of Horus.

Shen: the coil of rope known by the french term 'cartouche' - the Egyptian term derived from word meaning to encircle. Symbol of eternity and protective device around the name of the king.

Sycamore, Lady of the Southern: epithet of Hathor at Memphis, she had assisted Horus when blinded by Seth.

Tê: the underworld

Temhu: a town associated with the myth of 'Deliverance of Mankind'.

Teshtesh (see Griffin)

Thebes: during the 18th Dynasty (ca.1550 - 1295BC), the city of Weset was founded by Amenhotep I; better known by its Greek name, Thebes, it became the heart of the country. It was at this time that the Great Temple of Amon in Karnak became the country's most important religious centre and the royal necropolises were excavated in the Valley of the Kings and the

Valley of the Queens. *Theban Triad*: Amon-Ra, Mut and Khonsu.

Index

A
Aabt-offerings 119, 121, 139, 144
Abydos 110, 114, 118, 129
accidents 90
Adam 24
adze 28
Africa 180
  Sudan 21, 47
  West 21
Agathadaemon 16
age
  longevity 63
  old 26, 119, 131
  pre-dynastic 155
  primordial 113
air
  empty 154
Aken 21
Akhenaten 16, 31
Akhw 12, 20, 21, 25, 26, 46, 47, 113, 121, 140. *See also* spirits (akhw)
Akh ikher en Ra 29, 30
  becoming 40, 41
  cunning 30, 39
  drive away 41
  Fear of 21
  Panacht Stele 29
  spiritualised (sAX) 20
Alexandria 16, 150
Almanac of Lucky & Unlucky Days 9, 40, 50, 57, 62, 84, 95, 96
Amenhotep I 183
Amon 173
Amuletic Decrees 84–85
amulets 85, 143
Amun 16, 92, 94
Anat 173
ancestor
  cult 39
  family portrait 30
  father and mother 140
  spirits 46
androgyny 31
anger 136
Anhur 180
Ankh 65, 173
Ankhew 12
Ankhew, Akhew & Neterew 12–14
Ankh-tawi 106, 173
Anubis 67, 105, 122, 127, 173
  feast of 141
apartheid 151
Apophis 100, 114, 122, 126, 131, 138, 173. *See also* children: children of Bedesh (Apophis)
archaic burial 107
archangels 16
arrows
  from heaven 51
ascend 55
ashes 24
Ashmunein 110, 119

Ass. *See* donkey
assault
  supernatural 12, 84
Assmann, Jan
  Search for God in Ancient Egypt. 18
Astarte 174
astrology 57, 84
Ate 174
Atete 49
Atum 21, 122, 129
Ausim 50

B
Ba 20, 22
  generative force 20
  'Jiva' 20
  soul 20
Baba/Babai 131, 174
  red eared Baboon 102
Baboon 91
Babai
  red eared
  Baboon. *See also* Baba/Babai
Babylon 57, 84
Bak (servant) 90
Ban 26
Banebdjedet 130, 174
  the lusty bull 110
Bastet 19, 106, 111, 114, 117, 119, 125, 183
Bata
  ears of 113
Bebon 174
beer 32, 61, 63, 141, 174

Benben 114
Beni Hassan 25
Berber 176
Biat (wonder) 51, 87
Bible 22
  Joseph 57
birds 20, 46, 102, 134
birth 71
  newborns 90
  omen 131
bites & stings 90
black 144
blood 18, 26, 46, 49, 55, 64, 65, 69, 154, 156, 177
  impure 156
blue 36
Blue Lily (Nymphaea caerulea) 30
  Alabama farmers 33
  chalice 36
  peduncles 36
  roots 32
  Sacred Weeds 30
  'under the lotus' 33
  wrongly identified 32
boat 93, 108, 174
  mandjet 103
  mesektet 118, 140
  neshmet 114
  night 67
  prow of 106
  repulsion of the crew 139
body
  abdomen 93
  hand shaking 137
  mouth 92
  phallus 20, 154
  putrefaction 20
  rectum 93
  reversal 46, 155

shins 93
stature 63
teeth 70, 71
thighs 93
toes 93
vulva 20
Book of the Dead 72
Books of the beginning of the year 91
Books of the end of the year 91
Booze 32
Bori 21, 23
  leopard societies 22
  ridden 49
  ridden by 26
  Treamearne, A J N 21
brain 22
branding 63
bread 40, 141
  and beer 107
  pesen 61
breath 38
Budapest Museum of Fine Arts 85
bull
  of Meroe 174
  trampling of 101, 129, 137, 139
Bull of Ombos 40, 46, 51
Busiris 108, 126, 127, 174
Byblos
  King of 65

C

Cain 49
Cairo Calendar. *See* Almanac of Lucky & Unlucky days
cakes of light 15, 146. *See also* cakes of light

Calendar
  Lunar 10, 36, 40
cannibalism 22, 40, 51
canopic jars 66, 174
cardinal directions 16
Carthage 85
cartouche 174
cattle 123, 127. *See also* Bata
  neolithic cult 65
cave 126
Chaîne Opératoire 57
chanting 118
chaos 158
  magick 150
children 93
  adoption 67
  childlessness 67
  children of Bedesh (Apophis) 105, 107, 129, 138
  children of Nut (epagomenal days) 134
  of Geb and Nut 141
  of the storm 111
  youth 67
Christian 49
  clergy 22
  fanaticism 151
coffin
  texts **175**
consciousness 63
Constellations
  Great Bear 51
  fear of the seven stars 90
  seven stars 91
  Orion 101
Coptic 38, 123, 148
corn mummy. *See* Neper
crocodile 19, 100, 102, 107

crown
  Atef 174, 180
Culpepper, Nicholas 34

D
Damanhur 175
dance 22. *See also* Zar
day
  12 provinces of 174
  break 158
  darkness 125
  epagomenal 143
  special 40
  twilight 36
Dead, the 21, 66, 125, 176
  undead 20
death 26, 28, 33, 91
  in foreign lands **106**
Decans 8, 84, 86, 87, 93, 134
  Orion 127
decapitation 135, 156
Deir el Medina 28, 96, 151
demon 18, 47
  attack 71
  dancing 26, 50
  emissary 152
  Hayety 19
  of a canal 94
  of her father 94
  Secherou 38
  Shemay 19, 92
Dendara 176
Dep 109, 126, 133, 134
desert 93
diabolè/diabolic 147, 152
Dioscorides
  De Materia Medica 33
disease & medicine 18, 32, 47, 90, 91, 92, 119, 130

blindness 91, 140
entities 18, 21
fever 92
healing 67
heart 34
inoculation 26, 38
Islamic physicians 34
leprosy 91
pestilence 111, 118
phylactery 70, 154
physicians 33
skin rash 105, 134
therapy 33, 159
dismemberment 46, 110
disorder 91
divination. *See* omens
Djed pillars 111, 121, 176
Djesert 126
djet 20
dog 19, 118
  black 69
dolphin 115
donkey 154, 155
  Ass 69, 70
  Typhon's skull 69
dreams 9, 33, 40, 41, 71. *See also* evil: sleep
  lecherous 33
  night terrors 11
  of women 59
  vivid 33
drugs
  hallucinations 33
  Heroin 33
  mandrake 31, 34
  Micky Finn 34
  morning glory 34
  narcotic 30, 32
  Rohypnol 33
drunkenness 17, 62, 97, 105
Duat 36, 100, 102

E
eating 50
  dying breath 22
  eucharist 40
  food 26
  magick 38
Edfu 175
Egypt 24
  language 176
emissaries 96
Ennead 178
epagomenal days 176. *See also* children: children of Nut (epagomenal days)
Esna 95
Ethiopia 47
Eve 24
evil 9, 55, 91, 158
  colour 92
  dead 51
  eye 91
  personification of 155
  sleep 12, 60, 151, 152
execration rite 41
executioners (flowercutters) 96, 100, 122
  of Ra 119
  seven 122
executioners of Sekhmet 133
exorcism 48
eye
  Akhet 135, 136
  fugitive 137
  Horus the Elder 127
  of Horus 140
  of the undead 91
  Wedjat 105, 122, 128, 130, 134,

135, 140

F

family 94
fate 71, 84
feasts/festivals 18, 40
  Jubilation 105
  of your god 140
feeding
  the gods 138. *See also* eating
ferryman 110
fetish 28
filth 61
fire 137
  walking 55. *See also* feasts/festivals
fish 102, 114, 115, 134
flail 180
flower 32, 34
  cutters 19
folk 16, 17. *See also* Rekhyt
  underdogs 66
fossil
  Nerinea Requieniana 52
Freud, Sigmund 58
Fries, Jan
  Seidways 47
funeral
  bouquets 31
  cult 27

G

Geb 127
ghosts 14, 45, 47. *See also* Akhw
gifts 49
gnosis 11
goddess
  four noble ladies 15
  three noble ladies 112
gods
  assumption of 41
  Ennead 91
  fear of 19
  flighting 135
  local 107, 121
  minor 18
  of the day 117
  plague us 152
  safe from 92
  savage 65
  snake 85
  tying of the throats 135
gold 179
graphiti 150
Greek Magical Papyri 68, 148. *See* Papyrus Graecae Magicae
Greeks 33, 84, 151
green 144

H

hag 7
Hapy 120
Harpokrates 177
harpoon 103
Hathor 19, 65, 85, 100, 109, 114, 176, 177
  counting by names 133
  emissaries 19
  great book of fate 19
  hayty-demon 92
  seven 19
  white one 130
Hausa 21, 176
hawthorn 46
heart 15, 50, 63, 92
Hebrews 34, 57
  captivity 57
Hedj-hotpe 114

Hefau 119
Heliopolis 106, 111, 122, 124, 128, 129
herbs 30, 61
Hermetic Order of the Golden Dawn 11
Herodotus 84, 156
Hinduism 97
  Dakini 47
  tantra 47
  Yogini 47
Hippopotamus 64, 85
histeriola 177
honey 119
horizon
  doorways 112, 126
  eastern 121
horoscope 84
Horus 50, 60, 102, 103, 111, 122, 124, 130, 133, 142, 177
  & Seth 102, 109, 112, 119
  as Hippos 97
  Behadit 175
  crown
    white 112
  feast of 126, 130
  Four Sons 21, 51, 90
  Hekenu 117
  House of 97
  Letopolis 52
  the Elder 55, 105, 127, 128, 137, 142
Horus & Seth 55, 59, 103
  Battlefield 33, 120
  fighting 124
house 30
  foundation 108
  holy 131, 141

of Ra 97, 100, 130
Hu/Hw 105, 117, 119, 142

I
Iathath 177
Ibis 110
  Crested 25, 26
ideogramme 177
incense 120, 127, 133
incubi 18
Ipet-hemet (Hippo) 136
iron 22, 51, 178
  meteoric 90
Isis 16, 59, 64, 111, 122, 142, 143
  knot 65
Isis and Nephthys
  Lamentations 67, 118

J
jewelry 85
  bracelets 85
judgement 63, 124
  accusation 91
Juey 148, 151

K
Ka 20
karma 84
Karnak 125, 183
Khapesh 51
Khem 50
Khenti-irty 50, 117, 122
Khenty-Khem 50
Khepra 31, 128
khet 20
Khmun 178
Khnum 124
Khonsu 19, 31, 85, 91, 92, 173
kiki 176

King 65
  killing 22
  monarchy 155
  white crown 106
Kush 176

L
l. p. h. (life, prosperity and health 102, 127
ladder 53
  Jacob's 52, 178
  stairway to heaven 53
Lady of Heaven 174
lakes 94
  temporary 179
lamps 9
  nightlights 15
language
  code 152
  paronomasia 58
  popular usage 85
  puns 58
lapwing 66
leopards 22
Letopolis 90, 115, 122, 125, 131, 139, 142
  Foremost of Khem 50
letters 40
Letters to the Dead 39, 37
library 151
lion 85, 103, 107, 113, 115, 134, 135, 140
Littmann, Enno 47
liturgy 147
living
  and the dead 39
  needs of 87
lizards 107
luck 84
Luxor 90

lyet 122

M
Maat 92, 117, 122, 131, 137, 179
Maat heru - speaking true 179
navigation of 121
magic 11, 33. *See also* eating: magick
  freeform 9, 16, 152
  heka 18, 28
  Hermeticism 10
  initiation 20
  invocation 154
  magician (hery hebt) 28
  mistress of 143
  private 16, 87, 155
  sorcerers 36
  spell
    kit 151
  talismanic 49
  techniques 39
  threefold law 152
  warlock 94
  wax dolls 155
Mahes 117
man
  normal 60
  plebian 60
Maner 139
Manjet boat 174
marks 63
marriage
  batchelor 62
  bridesmaids 23
  veil 23
meditation 36
Mehit 180
Memphis
  Theology 68
Mendes 174
Menit 85, 86

Mercury 8
Mesektet 103, 111
Mesket boat 174
Mesolithic 180
Mesopotamia 58
meteorites 85, 178
milk 119
Min 123
   feast 141
   into the tent 127
Mithras
   Franz Cumont's
      Mysteries of
      Mithra 148
   Liturgy 150
Mnevis 122
Montu 92, 105, 128
moon
   god 19
mother 94
motherhood 65,
   67. *See also* birth
mourners 66
murder 151
musician
   goddess 101
Mut 92, 173, 179
   in Shera 138
myrrh 61, 127
myths 96

N

name 41
Napoleon 32
narcotic. *See also* Blue
   Lily (Nymphaea
   caerulea)
necropolis 183
Nefertem 117
Nehebkau 117
Nehes 179
Neith 102, 105, 107,
   114, 124, 135,
   182
   letter writing 122

Nekhbet 94
nekhekh - flail 180
Nemty 21, 110
Nephthys 56, 59, 67,
   69, 111, 142,
   143
   Beautiful of face 143
   crone 69
   domestic service 69
   housewife 68
   nursing 67
   old woman 70
   red cloth of 72
   sister 67
Neterew 12, 179
Nile 94, 180
   High 100
   inundation 30
Nome 179
nomen 180
Nubia 179
Nuit 61
   who counts the days
   125
Nun 96, 107, 118,
   120, 125
   his cavern 140

O

oath 119
Ombos. *See* Nagada
omens
   divination 41
   in the sky 100
   ironic reversals 58
On 180
Onnophris 129, 137
   in Sais 111
Onnophris in Sais 180
Onuris 180
Opening the Mouth 27
Opet 90
oracles 17, 51, 87,
   92. *See also*
   omens

Osiris 85, 96, 118,
   121, 122, 133,
   142, 155, 180
   Abydos 126
   corn-king 155
   feast 106, 114
   House of 97, 100
   Khenty 134
   The sheep 85
Osorkon 87
Ostraca 12
   Spell 46
Ostrich 179
Ovid 46

P

pagan 148
Palaeolithic 180
papyrus 12
   medical 32
Papyrus Brooklyn
   Magical 47
Papyrus Ebers 32
Papyrus, Leiden Magical
   34
Papyrus London-Leiden
   149
Papyrus Ramessium 68
Papyrus Turin Erotic
   33
pawt-cake 118
Pega the gap 180
phallus
   erect 173
Pharaoh 47
philosophy 72
   dialogue 60
   symposia 36
piety
   personal 17, 87
pigs 33
pilgrimage 92
Plato 9
Plutarch 65
poison 32

portal 140
priest 16, 18, 150
  hery heb or lector
    priest 18
  Sem 18
  sem 183
  temple 19
privileged 96
psychology 57
  animus/anima 59
  Id 9
  introvert 67
  Self 20
Ptah 85, 112, 117, 121, 141, 182
Ptah-Sokar-Osiris 129
pylon 182

R

Ra 41, 61, 96, 158, 182
  crew of 133
  Pre 181
  Pre-Harakhti 181
  setting 129
Ra Horakhty 100, 144
race & ethnicity 59
Ramesses II 64, 87
rebellion 122, 125, 131, 134, 137
red 62
  clay 15
  Goddess 68, 127
  ochre 154
Rekhyt 17, 18, 51, 60, 64, 66, 68, 90, 147, 155
Rennutet 111
Rome
  empire 147
  Legions 33
  Nero 33
Rostau 118, 139

S

sacrifice
  human 22
Sais 175, 178, 179
scepter
  Was 122
sceptre 180
seasons
  Peret 95, 124, 127
Secherou 47
secret 20
Sed 52, 95
Sekhmet 91, 103, 114, 117, 118, 119, 122, 129, 138, 182
Selket 36
Semitic 176
Senmut 85
Seth 21, 39, 51, 56, 58, 61, 62, 68, 103, 106, 107, 114, 121, 122, 140, 142, 143, 146, 149, 155, 159. *See also*
  Horus & Seth
  blue Lily 31
  Companions of 60
  Confederates of 103, 121, 122, 128, 140
  decapitation 106
  desert land 111
  headless 68
  ladder of 178
  name of 125, 129
  red one 112
  son of Nut 128
  Swy Heracleopolitan nome 128
  Typhon 152
Sethians 15, 66
Setna 183

Sety I
  temple of 150
  tomb of 8
sex 15, 18, 46, 47, 58
  homosexual 105
  intercourse 105, 117
  nocturnal emissions 34
  rape 47
Shabaka Stone 72
Shadrach, Meshach and Abednego 55
Shecha 47. *See also* Zar: cults
Shed 183
Shu 111, 118, 134, 135
Sia 105, 117
Sirius. *See* Sopdu (Sirius)
sixteen. *See* day of rams
sky
  If you see anything 101, 104, 105, 108, 113, 114, 118, 119, 121, 122, 123, 124, 129, 135, 138
sleep 34. *See also* evil: sleep
  three days 36
smell 24, 32, 106, 127
Smenkara 31
smoke 24
snake 19, 108, 140
  fire spitting cobra 101
Sobek 102, 129, 131, 135
  tongue of 107
Sokar 141, 180, 182
songs 118

Sopdu (Sirius) 139
Sothis. *See* Sopdu (Sirius)
spirits (akhw) 23, 60, 107, 113, 116, 118, 121, 125, 129. *See also* Akhw
  at birth 23
  Daemona 20
  feeding 28, 40
  Holy Guardian Angel 20
  Holy Guardian Angel. 23
  nature 22
  pact 40
  servitor 45
  thought form 45
Staatliche Museum, Berlin 31, 86
star
  going forth of 127
  imperishable 20, 55
  magick 50
Stele Panakht 30. *See also* Akhw: Panacht Stele
succubi 18
sun
  god. *See also* Ra
  midday 114, 141
  rise 152
  set 152
  symbolism 36
  visible 31
Sw 128
sycamore 183
symbolism 147

T

Tale of the Doomed Prince 19
Tale of Two Brothers 19
Tanenet 112, 117
Temhu 129
temple
  inaccessible 113
  kri- shrines 134
  ritual 17, 125
  rules broken 156
Thebes 87, 173, 183
Thoth 105, 117, 119, 124, 131, 135
thunderbolt 91
Thutmose III 52
tourism 150
trapezoid 182
tree 126
  holy 106
Tutankhamen 31
Typhon 149, 152, 155. *See also* Seth
Typhonian 50, 59, 62, 66

U

Ursa Major. *See* Great Bear

V

Valley of the Kings 183
Valley of the Queens 184
Vampires 9, 18, 40
  kiss 47, 147
  Lamia 46
  Mormos 46
  Striges 46
Venus 8
violence
  Do not beat anybody 136
  massacre 136
voice
  raising 123
  speech 66
Voodoo 49

W

wabet 105, 107, 122
Wag 40
Wainwright, Gerald Averay 55
warfare 64
weaving
  god 105
  goddess 101, 114
well 94
Weset 183
wine 32, 34
witchcraft 9, 47, 66, 94
women 65
work
  days 96

Y

yellow 36
Yin / Yang 59

Z

Zar 47–50
  cults 47
  dancers 26
  Horse of 49
  Shecha Zakiya 47
  Zara 48
zodiac 84

Spot any mistakes or want to offer some constructive feedback? The subject matter of this book is complex and inevitably there will be errors of transcription and understanding. In addition some of the ritual material undergoes natural revision by repeated use. Contact the author via the publishers and in return receive an update on work in progress, access to revisions plus a free gift.

Write C/O

Mandrake of Oxford
PO Box 250
OXFORD
OX1 1AP (UK)

Or search for Mandrake or Mogg Morgan on the Internet.

The Bull of Ombos: Seth & Egyptian Magick II

£12.99, ISBN 978-1869928-872, 356pp, 80 b&w illustrations

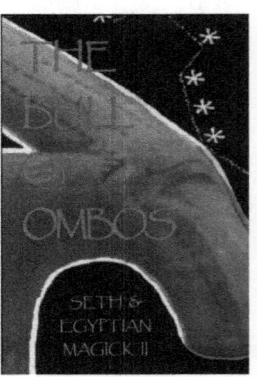

Naqada is town in Upper Egypt that gives its name to a crucial period in the prehistory of Egypt. In 1895, William Matthew Flinders Petrie, the 'father' of Egyptian archaeology, stumbled upon a necropolis, belonging to a very ancient city of several thousand inhabitants. Petrie's fateful walk through the desert led him to a lost city, known to the Greeks as Ombos, the Citadel of Seth. Seth, the Hidden God, once ruled in this ancient place before it was abandoned to the sands of the desert. All this forbidden knowledge was quickly reburied in academic libraries, where its stunning magical secrets had lain, largely unrevealed, for more than a century - until now.

This book is for all Egyptophiles as well as anyone with an interest in the archaic roots of magick and the sabbatic craft.

Contents: Gold in the desert / Sethians & Osirians / Cannibalism / Temple of Seth / Seth's Town / Bull of Ombos / Hathor / The names / Animals / the red ochre god / Seth and Horus / Opening the mouth / Seven / The Boat / Heka & Hekau / Magical activities / Cakes of Light / Magick and the funeral rite / Re-emergence of the Hidden God / Appendices / Extended bibliography / Glossary

Tankhem:
Seth & Egyptian Magick Vol I

£12.99, isbn 978-1869928-865, 234pp, second revised edition

The Typhonian deity Seth was once worshipped in Ancient Egypt. Followers of later schools obliterated Seth's monuments, demonised and neglected his cult. A possible starting point in the quest for the 'hidden god' is an examination of the life of Egyptian King Seti I ('He of Seth') also known as Sethos.

Contents: Prolegomena to Egyptian magick; Setanism; Tankhem; Egyptian Magick and Tantra; Sexual Magick; Twenty Eight; North; The Crooked Wand.

Orders to: Mandrake, PO Box 250, Oxford, OX1 1AP (UK)
Tel +44 (01865) 243671
email Mandrake@mandrake.uk.net
www.mandrake.uk.net

www.ingramcontent.com/pod-product-compliance
Lightning Source LLC
Chambersburg PA
CBHW032254150426
43195CB00008BA/454